THE MOST INSPII
STORIES

15

AMAZING & INSPIRING
TRUE TALES

FROM SOCCER'S GREATEST
GOALKEEPERS, DEFENDERS &
MIDFIELDERS

TERRENCE ARMSTRONG

CONTENTS

INTRODUCTION

Goalkeepers, defenders, & midfielders are often overlooked as they don't generally score the goals and create stunning finishes. (There are some exceptions). However, their role is vital to any soccer team.

We're going to take a look at 15 of the greatest goalkeepers, defenders, & midfielders. Many of them have experienced ups and downs on the field but have ultimately been triumphant, making a significant impact to the beautiful game.

Their determination, performance, and ethos should inspire you. They're lessons you can use throughout life, whatever you want to do, especially if you want to become an inspirational soccer player!

ERIC ABIDAL
STOPPING THE GREAT
CRISTIANO RONALDO

Eric Abidal was born in France in 1979 in Saint-Genis-Laval, a suburb of Lyon. Little is known about his early years although his family were devout Catholics.

Abidal discovered a passion for football at a young age and joined his local amateur team, AS Lyon Duchère in 1996. However, unlike many of his soccer-crazy friends, Abidal had a real passion for defense.

The four years he spent playing amateur football honed his skills and brought him to the attention of Monaco. He joined the Monaco B team in 2000 and made his professional league debut the same year, helping AS Monaco FC defeat Toulouse 3-0.

Despite his potential, Abidal only played in 22 games across two seasons, encouraging him to move to Lille in 2002. This allowed him to reunite with his former manager Claude Puel. Between 2002 and 2004 Abidal was first-choice in defense. It's this that gave him the confidence to grow and become one of the best defenders in the world.

In 2004 he was transferred to Lyon and was instrumental in the team winning three national championships, back-to-back! In short, attackers just couldn't get past him. Even the great Cristiano Ronaldo struggled with Abidal's defensive skills.

As Abidal said "As a defender, my aim is to infuriate the opponent. I want him to be so sick of the sight of me that he has to move somewhere else on the field to get away."

It's this mentality, the relentless coverage of opponents that made Abidal special.

During his time at Lyon, he even scored his first goal.

Unfortunately, soccer is a tough game. Abidal fractured his metatarsus early in the 2005-2006 campaign. He took time to recover but still managed to play in 15 games throughout the season.

By 2007 he had transferred to FC Barcelona for an impressive €9 million. This was part of Barcelona's golden years. By 2010 the team had become the first Spanish team to ever win six trophies in one year.

He stayed with Barcelona for six years and faced his biggest challenge off the field. It was serious enough to threaten his ability to play professionally again.

In 2011 Abidal was diagnosed with a tumor in his liver. Within two days of it being discovered he had surgery and messages of support flooded sports websites and social media.

The surgery appeared to be a success. At the end of May 2011, he played the full match against Manchester United. Helping Barcelona win the Champions League again. As a mark of respect, the team captain, Puyol, gave him the captain's armband and let him be the first player to pick up the trophy.

It was noted throughout the rest of the season that Abidal's play wasn't at the same level as before. He still gave it his all on the field, but by March 2012 the unresolved issues meant he needed a liver transplant.

Fortunately, his cousin was a match, Abidal underwent surgery in April and was allowed out of hospital in May.

In a show of dedication, Abidal started training again as soon as October. However, the strain of training took its toll and he paused, stating he wanted to focus on recovery first. He officially started training again in January 2013 and played his first game for Barcelona in March, managing 65 minutes on the field.

By the end of April, he was playing the full 90 minutes and was, once again, considered a dangerous force on the field. In fact, Abidal continued to play professionally until 2020, when he finally retired.

Abidal's story isn't just about recovering from illness and returning to form. He achieved a huge amount during his career and became an inspiration to others on and off the field.

Part of this was recognized in the 67 appearances he made for the French national team. He first played for them in 2004, but his starring moment was really the 2006 FIFA World Cup.

Abidal was selected for the national squad and played in every match of the tournament except when France played Togo. He wasn't allowed to play after receiving two yellow cards in the previous games, effectively suspending him from the match.

He was instrumental in the final between France and Italy, which went to penalties after a 1-1 draw. He was selected to take one of the penalties and scored. Unfortunately, it wasn't quite enough and France lost to Italy that year.

Abidal played for France in several other tournaments, including the Euro 2008 qualifying campaign, and the 2010 World Cup, but France didn't achieve the same level of success as in 2004.

Throughout his career, he won eight league titles and multiple other trophies at club level. While his play post-surgery was never quite the same as pre-surgery. He was still seen as an extremely capable player, as strong as an ox and fast. Enough to worry any attacker.

Interestingly, his love for the game has never subsided. Despite the ups and downs of his career Abidal remains dedicated to the beautiful game and improving its image across the globe.

As such, he took on an ambassador role for Barcelona to promote the club's values, and soccer in general, across the globe.

FUN FACTS ABOUT ABIDAL

- His first of 67 appearances for the French national team was on 18 August 2004
- Abidal was the first choice during the Euro 2008 qualifying campaign
- He opted out of the 2010 World Cup game when France played the host country, South Africa
- He could play as a left-back or center
- Abidal converted to Islam in his early 20s

QUICK TRIVIA TEST

When did Abidal join AS Lyon Duichère?

1996

How long did Abidal play for Barcelona?

6 years

What illness stopped Abidal from playing in 2012?

A liver tumor

How far did France get in the 2004 World Cup?

They were runners-up

How many league titles did he win in his career?

Eight

FIVE LIFE LESSONS

Believe in yourself

In 2002 Abidal transferred to Lille and flourished, simply because his manager believed in him and gave him the chance to become a great player.

That belief was simply a catalyst. The truth was, that it encouraged Abidal to believe in himself and unlock his full potential.

Believe in what you're capable of and unlock your full potential!

Know when it's time to quit

Abidal chose to retire during his first season with Olympiacos after playing just nine games. As he said, "A top-level athlete is the only one who can know to stop their career, and for me, it is time."

In short, he got to go out at the top because he knew it was the right time to quit, for his health and his reputation.

Knowing when to quit is important in all walks of life. Quitting means accepting you've achieved everything you can or you've learned from the mistakes of failure and are ready to move on and try again. It doesn't mean giving up because things have got difficult.

Support comes from unexpected places

When Abidal was faced with a liver tumor he found support from his teammates and soccer fans. It wasn't just being given the captain's armband.

Both teams in the round-of-16 Champions League match in 2011 wore t-shirts saying "Animo Abidal" which means Get well Abidal. The fans in the Barcelona match against Getafe CF clapped for the entire 22nd minute. (22 was his shirt number).

Never be afraid to share issues, you may be surprised at where support comes from.

Find your own destiny

It's tempting to follow the herd or do something because others have told you it's a good idea. However, as Abidal once said, "Everyone has their own destiny."

Think about what's important to you and follow your heart, this will help you find your own destiny.

You can do anything

No matter how impossible something may seem, you can do it if you put your mind to it. That's the attitude Abidal had to help him recover from liver surgery It worked for him and can work for you too.

AARON RAMSEY
THE PLAYER WHO TURNED
DOWN MANCHESTER UNITED

Aaron Ramsey was born in Wales in December 1990 and started playing soccer at school. Today he is known as one of the best midfielders in the world, although he'll occasionally play on the left or right wing.

What's surprising is that he didn't start playing football until he was nine years old. That's old compared to a lot of the best footballers in the world!

Fortunately, Ramsey has a natural talent. He was also already athletic as he was a keen rugby player.

He started out playing in the local youth development program. It was at this time that he was approached by St. Helens, a rugby league team.

Ramsey had already signed to Cardiff City's youth academy, so went with soccer as his sport of choice.

It was a wise choice, he excelled in training and Cardiff City signed him to their professional team. He had his first taste of the professional league when he played the last minute of Cardiff City's game against Hull City on 28 April 2007. It may seem like a small achievement but it made him the youngest player to ever play for Cardiff City! He was 16 years and 124 days old.

He signed a contract with Cardiff later the same year, it was the beginning of an impressive career.

The following January he was nominated for the Player of the Round, primarily due to his performance for Cardiff against Chasetown.

A few months later the talented midfielder scored his first professional goal and started to become a regular in the first team. His first full season saw him play 22 games, including five FA Cup match games, Cardiff only played six games.

His performance during Cardiff's FA Cup run meant that Manchester United tried to persuade him to join them. It was an offer that Ramsey turned down. Instead, in 2008, the clubs confirmed that Ramsey would be moving to Arsenal. They paid $5 million upfront.

It's worth noting that Ramsey chose Arsenal because their approach was more personal. The Arsenal manager flew Ramsey and his family to Switzerland to discuss what they envisioned for his future.

2008 saw Ramsey start to show his impressive abilities. In the first few months, he assisted in several goals and scored his first goal in the group stages of the UEFA Champions League. It made him the second player born in the 1990s to score a Champions League Goal. A strange claim to fame!

Ramsey continued to play well, exceeding Arsenal's expectations. Unfortunately, a tackle in February 2010 caused a double fracture in Ramsey's leg. It was a month later before he started walking, with the aid of crutches.

He didn't train with the team again until October 2010.

The next couple of years were tough for the star. He was loaned to Nottingham Forest and then to Cardiff City. Both teams were grateful for his skills and he used the slightly less stressful environment to maximize his fitness and form.

Due to his injury and adverse weather, he only played five games for Nottingham Forest. He fared better with Cardiff City and played in several games. A minor thigh injury caused a hiccup in his recovery process.

It was March 2011 before he made a start for Arsenal again. However, he had an excellent season, assisting in several goals and scoring in several matches himself.

However, what the team really noticed was the difference in his mentality. As Cardiff's boss said "It really was a case of someone leaving as a boy and coming back as a man....He is so strong mentally."

The process of dealing with his serious injury helped Ramsey increase his mental endurance and helped him become a better player on the field.

Alongside several assists, Ramsey scored a dramatic and impressive last-minute winner against Marseille in the Champions League group stages. It was just one of several impressive goals marking his return to Arsenal.

The fans also saw the difference, they voted him Man of the Match twice and Player of the Month.

But, even this was just a hint of what was to come. The 2013-2014 season was perhaps his best ever. He scored in the first leg of the Champions League play-off and claimed another Man of the Match. That's a title he earned more than once that season. He also got voted Player of the Month four months running.

Ramsey performed so well that Wenger moved him into a new deeper midfield role. It suited his playing style perfectly, leading to several inspired performances. That's assists and goals.

His excellent form came into play at the end of the season, allowing him to score a goal at long range against Liverpool. It gave Arsenal the victory and put them five points clear at the top of the Premier League.

Ramsey continued to play at the highest level for Arsenal until 2019 when he signed a four-year contract with Juventus. Since then, he has played for Juventus and been loaned to Rangers, before transferring to Nice in 2022.

One thing is certain, if Ramsey is on the field, anything can happen.

Of course, Ramsey has also played for the Welsh team. He was first called up in 2005 to the U17s. He also played for the U21s, then started for the Welsh national team in 2008. He even scored a goal in the 2010 World Cup qualifier.

Ramsey was also asked to play in a friendly against Scotland. Wales won 3-0 and he assisted with all three goals.

In recognition of his talent, Ramsey was made team captain on 26 March 2011. At 20 years and 90 days old he became the youngest Welsh soccer captain ever.

Ramsey was there and assisted with the goal in Wales's first win in a major international tournament for 58 years! They built Slovakia 2-1. By the end of the 2014 FIFA World Cup, he had the joint-highest number of assists for the tournament.

There is little doubt that for team and country, Ramsey became known as one of the most influential players on and off the field.

FUN FACTS ABOUT RAMSEY

- You can find Ramsey on Instagram under @aaronramsey
- Ramsey is a keen supporter of the World Wildlife Fund
- He's sponsored by Addidas
- Ramsey was the Welsh Schools' Athletic Association pentathlon champion in 2005
- He lived with his parents and brother until he moved to London, where he shared with Chris Gunter

QUICK TRIVIA TEST

At what age did Ramsey start playing football?

Nine

Which non-soccer club approached him when he was young?

St. Helens Rugby Club

How long did he play for in his debut professional game against Hull City?

One minute!

How old was he when he first played for Cardiff City?

He was 16 years and 124 days old

When did he first become Wales team captain?

26 March 2011

FIVE LIFE LESSONS

1. You're never too old (or too young)

In Ramsey's case, nine was comparatively old to start a football career. However, he succeeded through skill, hard work, and dedication.

These are the same attributes that anyone can use to become a success at something, no matter how old they are.

In short, don't let age get in the way, try it anyway.

2. Follow your passion

When Ramsey was young he was considered a top-athlete. He was the 2005 Welsh Schools' Athletic Association pentathlon champion and was offered an opportunity with a local rugby club.

Ramsey chose to follow his biggest passion, soccer and has never looked back.

You should do the same.

3. Go the extra Mile

Ramsey signed for Arsenal in 2008 because, despite having offers from lots of clubs, Arsenal went the extra mile.

They didn't just fly him to Switzerland to discuss his future, they made sure his family came too and every need was catered for.

Going the extra mile meant that they got their man.

4. Don't let injury get you down

Ramsey suffered a nasty broken leg in 2010 which stopped him from training until the end of the year. It could have signaled the end of his career. Instead, he persevered with his fitness and health program and eventually returned to form.

Injuries can happen at any time, you need to commit to making a full recovery and take enough time to do so.

5. Don't forget what matters

It's easy to get caught up in the hype. However, you also need to remember what really matters. For Ramsey, a seriously broken leg was enough for him to appreciate what he has and how easily it could be taken away.

It helped build his mental resilience and keep his feet on the ground.

Everyone should consider what is really important to them and focus on that. It will help you reach your full potential rather than relying on hype.

PETR CECH
STRIKER TURNED GOALKEEPER

Petr Cech was born in 1982 in Pizen, Czechoslovakia. He's one-third of a triplet, the other two-thirds are his brother Michal and sister Sarka. It's said he has a weaker skull than standard because he's a triplet.

Cech started playing soccer at a very early age, it was simply something he enjoyed. By age seven he was selected for the local team: Skoda Plzen. He initially played as a striker. However, when he was ten years old he broke his leg. When it healed he returned to the squad and tried out as a goalkeeper.

He found he wasn't just good at it, he had the potential to be one of the best. From then on, he trained as a goalkeeper.

By the time he was seventeen, he was ready to play professionally. He joined Chmel Blsany in June 1999 and played his first league game in October of the same year. The team lost 3-1, but it was enough for the Czech First League to see his talent.

The following year, Cech signed for Sparta Prague, starting with them at the beginning of the 2001-2002 season.

The 17th November 2001 was a memorable occasion for Cech. It was when Marcel Melecky scored a goal against him, the first goal Cech had conceded in 903 consecutive minutes of play! That's a record.

At this stage Arsenal was interested, but in July 2002, Cech moved to Rennes and earned his first Man of the Match. It could be argued that his goalkeeping skills saved the team from relegation, despite them being bottom of the league.

This was when Cech learned French, alongside his knowledge of Czech, English, German, and Spanish!

His reputation was growing rapidly and, in February 2004, Rennes accepted a deal from Chelsea worth £7 million, sending Cech into the English Premier League.

Chelsea already had a first-choice goalkeeper, Carlo Cudicini. Unfortunately, he suffered an elbow injury early in Cech's first season, allowing him to take over.

Cech showed the Premier League what a goalkeeper could do. By 5 March 2005, he had clocked 1025 minutes of consecutive gameplay without letting in a goal! He was given an award by the Premier League for the achievement.

Cech also received the Premier League Golden Glove for managing 24 games in one season without letting a goal in. He was certainly instrumental in Chelsea keeping the Premier League title.

It would seem things couldn't get much better for Cech. In 2005, he was named the World's Best Goalkeeper by IFFHS.

Unfortunately, his almost magical career took a tumble in October 2006, when Stephen Hunt collided with Cech in the penalty area, his knee hit the goalie in the head. Cech tried to play on but a few minutes later was forced to retire.

Interestingly, Cudicini replaced him and was knocked unconscious later in the same game!

Cech suffered a depressed skull fracture. While it didn't appear serious at first, if he delayed treatment any longer Cech could have died.

Cech was out of action for three months, allowing his skull to heal. For the rest of his career, he wore a headguard, similar to those available for rugby players.

Fortunately, Cech didn't lose his skills, although he had no memory of the incident. In his comeback game, Chelsea lost 2-0 to Liverpool. However, he then went on to play 810 minutes of consecutive play without conceding a goal. Not quite his record but still an impressive recovery.

His play was so good he was given the Premier League Player of the Month award, the first goalkeeper to get the award in seven years!

Chelsea won the 2007 FA Cup Final, aided by Cech not letting one goal in for the entire game.

Unfortunately, Cech's bad luck on the field wasn't over. In November 2007 he injured his calf muscle, in December of the same year it was his hip, and in training early in 2008 injured his ankle!

He missed several games and Chelsea's performance was affected. To top it off, he collided with Tal ben Haim on 7 April 2008 in a training session and needed surgery on his mouth and chin.

Cech bounced back again! He never stopped trying and impressing the team. In the first 17 games of the season, Chelsea only let 7 goals past them. No goals were scored against Chelsea in an impressive 11 of the 17 games, Cech was the keeper for 10 of the clean sheets.

By November, Cech reached the 100-match target. That's 100 matches while playing for Chelsea without conceding a goal! To complete his bounce-back he helped Chelsea secure the 2009 FA Cup Final, Cech's seventh trophy with the team.

Despite some ups and downs, Cech helped Chelsea keep the cup the following season.

Cech continued to play for Chelsea until 2015. He sported a few injuries and many clean sheets, consistently proving that he was the best goalkeeper in the world. By January 2014 he managed to acquire his 209th clean sheet for Chelsea. Unfortunately, a shoulder injury in April 2014 knocked him out for the rest of the season.

He started a new contract with Arsenal on 29 June 2015. Despite his impressive record, he was no longer the first-choice keeper at Chelsea, this made him feel it was the right time to move on.

That didn't stop him from excelling at Arsenal. He extended his Premier League clean sheet run and won the Premier League Goalkeeper of the season, as well as the Golden Glove.

His clean sheets continued until January 2019, when Cech announced his retirement from the beautiful game. His final game was on 29 May against his old side Arsenal.

FUN FACTS ABOUT CECH

- Cech is a keen musician and plays drums surprisingly well
- He speaks Czech, English, French, German, Italian, Spanish, and Portuguese
- Cech has one daughter and one son
- Cech holds Chelsea's record of 228 clean sheets
- Since retiring from soccer Cech has become a semi-professional ice hockey goaltender!

QUICK TRIVIA TEST

Why does Cech have a weak skull?

Because he's a triplet

How many consecutive minutes did Cech play without letting a goal in when playing for Chelsea?

1025 minutes!

Why did Cech change from being a striker to a goalkeeper?

Because he broke his leg when he was ten

Whose knee hit Cech in the head?

Stephen Hunt

Where was Petr Cech born?

Pizen, Czechoslovakia

FIVE LIFE LESSONS

1. Do the best with what you have

Cech was born with a weak skull. In other words, it's easier for him to damage his skull and possibly his brain than it is for others.

This could have been enough to persuade him not to play soccer, especially as a goalie. It didn't stop Cech. He's aware of the issue and takes precautions to protect his head while still doing the thing he loves the most.

That's a good attitude for anyone to have.

2. Explore all options

Sometimes the right path is the easiest one. Other times, the best path isn't always as clear. Cech is a perfect example of this. He played well as a striker and could have played the position professionally.

However, a broken leg made him reconsider and switch to a different path; as a goalkeeper. He wasn't just good at that, he was excellent.

In short, consider all your options before you pick one.

3. Safety First

Cech's head injury while playing for Chelsea caused many people in soccer, and connected to it, to call for better protection for keepers. It was something that didn't lead to any results.

However, Cech did wear the head guard for the rest of his career, illustrating to everyone why safety is important.

It's something you should learn from. Always put your safety first.

4. Never Be Afraid To Try New Things

Cech is a walking example of trying new things. He started as a striker and switched to being a keeper. After retiring from soccer, he changed sports to ice hockey, and he's tackled and learned a variety of foreign languages.

In short, he's prepared to try new things and you should be able to do the same.

5. Focus on what you can do better

Cech says "When I hit 100 clean sheets, and it was the fastest 100 as well, I thought, 'OK, that's an achievement in such a tough league.' But I am always thinking of the next milestone, can you do 150?"

It's that attitude which made him such a legendary goalkeeper and an attitude everyone should have.

JUAN ARANGO
THE GREATEST VENEZUELAN
SOCCER PLAYER EVER

Juan Arango was born in May 1980 in Venezuela, although his parents were both Colombian. He's generally regarded as the greatest Venezuelan soccer player ever. He spent most of his professional career playing in La Liga. Of course, he also played for the Venezuelan international side.

Although the son of immigrants, Arango had a fairly normal childhood. Like many of the children in his neighborhood, there wasn't much to do to pass the time. This was a period before the internet! As such, most of the children spent their time kicking balls around the streets.

It's how Arango discovered he had a talent for soccer, and enough passion to pursue it.

Of course, as a youngster, he had to balance schoolwork with soccer practice. His parents were supportive but also realistic. They knew how hard it was to become a professional soccer player and made sure he kept up with his studies while playing.

The good news for Arango was that he also had talent. He was scouted at an early age and asked to join the local soccer academy. By the time he was 16, he had joined Nueva Cadiz FC and was given a professional contract.

Interestingly, the team made it into the Venezuelan Primera Division just one year after he joined them They changed their name to Zuila FC. Although Arango was new to the team, he played an instrumental role in getting them into the league.

As an attacking midfielder, he had impressive instincts and seemed to always be just where he needed to be. It was a feat that didn't go unnoticed in the Venezuelan league. After just one year with Zuila FC, he moved across to Caracas FC, another league team.

However, that wasn't the end of his meteoric rise to fame. Just six months into his time with Caracas he was sold to Mexico's C.F. Monterrey.

That wasn't enough for the budding star. He was already becoming known in Venezuela and Mexico. His fame grew even more as he transferred between clubs in Mexico. He played for Monterrey for just one year before transferring to Pachuca for the 2002-2003 season. Arango scored an impressive 16 goals in one season with Pachuca. He played 52 games for them.

The following season, 2003-2004, he played for Puebla, another Mexican team.

His skills and the contacts he made over those years were instrumental to the next stage of his career. At the finish of the 2003-2004 season, Arango was approached by RCD Mallorca, a well-established and reputable side in the Spanish La Liga. The coach was Benito, who had been in charge when Arango was at Monterrey.

He was offered a one-year contract with an option to extend it by three more, depending on his play. Arango accepted and stayed with Mallorca from 2004-2009.

Mallorca was where Arango really started to shine. It's also where he faced his biggest challenge on the field.

It was March 20 2005 when Arango and Javi Navarro (playing for Sevilla FC) collided. Arango was knocked to the ground, swallowing his tongue, breaking his cheekbone, gaining multiple cuts on his face, and breaking his cheekbone.

You should note, it's not possible to actually swallow your tongue. However, it's a muscle and it can relax enough to block your airways, causing a lack of oxygen to your organs and brain. That can result in serious injuries.

Fortunately for Aragon, there were, as always in soccer games, medical experts standing by to help.

It took Aragon a month to recover before he returned triumphantly to the field. He still managed to score 11 goals during that season and was the top scorer for the team.

Arango continued to play for Mallorca and helped to produce some outstanding results. He scored 45 goals in his time with the team and appeared in 183 games.

In 2006 he was called the third best Latin American player in La Liga. He subsequently chose to get a Spanish passport, he officially got this in 2007.

Despite being an amazing player, Arango didn't manage to score a hat-trick until March 2008. Mallorca beat Recreativo de Huelva 7-1, Arango scored three of the goals.

As his contract with Mallorca was getting near to a close, Arango was sold to Borussia Monchengladbach. The fee was €3.6 million and the contract was three years. It allows Arango to move into the German league.

Amazingly, Arango's game improved further. He still played as an attacking midfielder but somehow he seemed even better at always being in the right spot.

He played with Borussia from 2009-2014, scoring 25 times out of 154 appearances. However, it was his goal in December 2012 that showed the world how great he really was. He shot the ball past the keeper from 48 yards out. It caused many people to call him the best left-footed player in the world.

He frequently ranked as the most popular soccer player in the world.

After a successful career, he returned to Mexico in 2014 to play for Tijuana. Surprisingly, it was in 2015, while playing for Tijuana, that he showed an uncharacteristic bad-boy side to his persona. He bit Jesus Zavaia during a game and earned a two-month ban.

Arango wound down his career by playing for the New York Cosmos in the North American Soccer League.

Internationally, he was first chosen to play in the Venezuelan side in 2004. He played for Venezuela in all three group-stage matches in the American Cup. 2007 turned out to be even better. He assisted in Venezuela's first-place finish in the group stages and even scored in the quarterfinals, although the national team lost to Uruguay.

2007 was also the year that he was made team captain for Venezuela. But, he wasn't done. In 2011 he led Venezuela to fourth place in the American Cup. That was the best result Venezuela has ever had in the championship. Arango played in 116 games for Venezuela and his 22 goals on the international stage holds the joint record for most goals scored by a Venezuelan player.

FUN FACTS ABOUT ARANGO

- Arango spent most of his professional career playing in La Liga for Mallorca
- He was capped by Venezuela 116 times
- Arango turned professional at 16
- He played two seasons with New York Cosmos but played for Zulia between those seasons
- He's considered the greatest Venezuelan soccer player of all time

QUICK TRIVIA TEST

Where were Arango's parents from?

Columbia

How long did he play for Caracas?

6 months

Which club did he play for between 2004 and 2009?

Mallorca

What happened to Arango in 2005 when he collided with Javi Navarro?

He lost consciousness and swallowed his tongue

When did he score his first hat trick?

March 2008

FIVE LIFE LESSONS

1. Be nice to people on the way up

In business people will often climb over each other trying to reach the top. However, those you climb over are likely to get revenge when you're on the way back down.

Instead, be nice to people on the way up and they'll help you when they can. It can make a big difference in life. It certainly did for Arango, his break into the Spanish soccer league was via his old coach.

2. Good things happen if you put yourself out there

Some people get spotted and get lucky. However, for most people, the secret to success is in being seen. Just as Arango got his big break into Spanish soccer via being seen by a coach, you can get your big break if you make sure people know what you're capable of.

3. Success doesn't always mean playing for the biggest clubs

Arango was frequently recognized as one of the best players in the world. Yet, despite offers, he chose to spend most of his career with Mallorca and Borussia.

Success for him was enjoying the game, not trying to secure a spot with a bigger club. That's a worthwhile approach to life, think about what is really important to you.

4. Your background doesn't define you

Arango had immigrant parents but he was born in Venezuela. He was accepted as a Venezuelan and represented the national team. In short, he wasn't defined by his immigrant parents, he made his own path.

You should do the same.

5. Never give up

Arango had a serious injury in 2005, one that could have ended his career. Instead, he focused on recovering and played with the team again just a month later. He even went on to become the top scorer that season.

I have included these free downloadable gifts to help light up your inner inspiration & reach your potential.

While you are reading through the stories, lessons and trivia, we recommend that you make use of all the bonuses we've attached here!

All our bonuses have been made specifically to help young athletes feel fired up, get inspired from the best to ever do it, and most importantly fall more in love with this incredible game!

Here's a list of what you're getting-

1) 250 Fun Facts From The World Of Sports
2) Sports Practice and Game Calendar
3) 5 Fun Exercise Drills for Kids
4) The BEST Advice From The Greatest Athletes Of All Time
5) The Mental Mindset Guided Meditation & Affirmation Collection
6) The Most Famous Events In Sports History And What They Can Teach Us

Now, it's over to you to scan the QR code, follow the instructions & get started!

DIEGO MARADONA
THE ARGENTINIAN LEGEND

Diego Armando Maradona was born in October 1960 and is generally seen as one of the greatest soccer players to ever grace the planet. His skills are legendary and he is one of just two winners of the FIFA World Player of the Century. It was a special award, held over two polls, to mark the turn of the century.

The joint winners were Pelé and Maradona. Both are an inspiration to young soccer players everywhere.

Maradona was born in Buenos Aires, the fifth out of eight children. His childhood was fairly typical of the time, he and his family lived in a poor neighborhood and were perhaps the poorest family in the area thanks to the number of children.

Despite having little, Maradona was gifted a ball by his cousin when he was three years old. To make sure it wasn't stolen Maradona slept with the ball inside his shirt! His family were pushing him to become an accountant until they realized how good he was with the ball.

At age nine, he joined the village soccer team, called "Little Onion", and his skill in dribbling, passing, and stunning footwork meant others quickly paid attention. Thanks to Maradona, the Little Onion's won 140 consecutive games. It is still regarded as the best youth team in Argentinian history

Just ten days before his sixteenth birthday, Maradona made his professional debut, playing for the Argentinos Juniors. He was the youngest player ever in the Argentine Primera division

Maradona didn't hold back and wasn't overawed by the occasion. Just a few minutes into the game he dribbled the ball through Juan Domingo Cabrera's legs, showcasing his talent and a move that would become one of his trademarks. Just two weeks later he scored his first goal in professional football.

Maradona spent five years with the Argentinos Juniors, honing his skills. He scored an impressive 115 goals from 167 appearances. Then he transferred to B oca Juniors for an impressive $4 million. He scored twice in his debut game.

Just one year later he moved to Barcelona, the transfer fee of $7.6 million set a new record at the time. He quickly showed the fans he was worth it, helping Barcelona win the Copa del Rey in 1983 and the Spanish Super Cup in the same year. He was even applauded by the Real Madrid fans for his skill. Maradona had dribbled past everyone, including the keeper. Madrid's defender came in with a sliding tackle and Maradona simply stopped, allowing the defender to slide past him. He then casually slotted the ball into the back of the net. Only two other opposition players have ever been applauded by the fans of Real Madrid!

Unfortunately, it wasn't all plain sailing at Barcelona. Maradona contracted hepatitis which stopped him from playing for a while. Worse, he was the victim of a reckless tackle when playing Athletic Bilbao. It broke his ankle and threatened to end his career.

Fortunately, after three months of rehabilitation, he returned to the field, his talent still clearly intact.

Other issues on the field included racism. There was a nasty fight during the 1984 Copa del Rey final in Madrid when Barcelona were playing Athletic Bilbao.

The Bilbao fans and one player, Miguel Sola, taunted Maradona throughout the game on account of his native American ancestry. Maradona snapped at full-time. He went head-to-head with Sola, exchanging expletives. Maradona then headbutted Sola, elbowed another, and kneed a third, knocking him unconscious. In return, a Bilbao player, Goikoetxea, kicked Maradona in the chest, and then both teams entered an all-out brawl. It was the last straw for Barcelona. They had already put up with Maradona's frequent disputes with the executives. Maradona was immediately transferred to Napoli. The transfer fee was an impressive $10.48 million.

It was a fantastic period for Maradona. His background resonated with the Southern Italian team. At the time there was a big divide between north and south Italy, the north was a lot wealthier. The South had never won a league title.

Maradona soon changed that! He joined them at the end of the 1983-84 season. By 1986 they had won the Serie A Italian championship. Southern Italy celebrated with impromptu street parties and burning mock coffins of northern teams.

The next three seasons saw the team win the league again and be runners-up twice.

Of course, Italy was less happy when Maradona, and the Argentinian team, beat Italy in the 1990 World Cup.

Alongside all this success, Maradona played for Argentina. He appeared 91 times for the national team and scored 34 goals. Strangely, he made his debut at 16 when Argentina played Hungary in 1977 but was left off the squad for the 1978 World Cup because the coach felt he was too young.

It was his performance in 1979, when Argentina played, and beat, Japan in the 1979 FIFA World Youth Championship, that is perhaps one of the most memorable in his career. Everyone who watched was left open-mouthed at the way he took the ball, moved with it, and dribbled around his opponents. He was an unstoppable force.

Of course, for Maradona, captaining the Argentinian team to World Cup victory in 1986 was one of his highlights. He played every minute in every game for Argentina and scored five goals. It's the tournament that is famous for having the goal scored by 'the hand of god', and by having the greatest goal in the history of the World Cup. Both were scored by Maradona.

FUN FACTS ABOUT MARADONA

- He was fouled 53 times in the 1986 World Cup, a record that has yet to be beaten
- Maradona has played in 21 World Cup matches, 16 of which were as Argentinian captain
- Maradona and Messi are the only soccer players to have won the FIFA Under-20 and Golden Ball titles in the FIFA World Cup
- In 2005 he launched a talk show called "The Night of the Number 10"
- In 2010, The Times newspaper in London placed Maradona number one in the top ten World Cup players of all time

QUICK TRIVIA TEST

How many brothers and sisters does Maradona have?

7

How many games did the Little Onion's win consecutively?

140

What illness did Maradona contract at Barcelona?

Hepatitis

How many goals did he score for Argentina

34

Why was Maradona left off the 1978 World Cup squad?

The coach felt he was too young

FIVE LIFE LESSONS

1. Don't let poverty hold you back

Maradona came from a poor background but he didn't let this stop him. Although he was naturally talented, it was his dedication to practice and his attitude that turned him into a star and a legend.

Being poor should never stop you from chasing your dreams.

2. Always look on the bright side

When Maradona broke his ankle it could have ended his career. Rest and the best rehabilitation specialists helped. But, to return from any injury like that, you need a positive attitude. Maradona always believed he would play again. It was that positive nature which helped him to return to the beautiful game.

3. Fighting achieves nothing

Maradona started the fight with Bilbao players at the end of the match. While the taunts were unfair, he could have chosen to walk away. Instead, he reacted and he never played for Barcelona again.

In short, violence isn't the answer, find a better solution.

4. Success is the result of hard work

Maradona had an incredible talent. However, he also spent hours practicing and honing his skills. As he himself said, "When people succeed, it is because of hard work. Luck has nothing to do with success."

In short, no matter how great your talent, work hard to get better.

5. Own up to your mistakes

Maradona once said, "I am Maradona who makes goals, who makes mistakes." He made a lot of mistakes in his life and didn't own up to all of them at the time. But, he did own up to them eventually.

The sooner you own up to your mistakes the easier it will be for you to move forward.

RUBEN DIAS
A FAMILY OF SOCCER PLAYERS

Ruben Dias was born in May 1997 in the district of Lisbon, Portugal. His nickname growing up was "Ruby" courtesy of his older brother Ivan. Interestingly, Ivan is also a professional soccer player.

As a child, Dias did what most of the other children in his neighborhood did, spent time playing football on the streets. It was an excellent way for him and his brother to bond.

His older brother had already joined the local soccer club, Estrela da Amadora and Dias followed suit, recommended by his brother.

When he first started to play for them he was positioned as a striker. However, after his team lost by two goals in one match, he was moved to defense. It helped to hone his skills.

In 2008, when he was just 11 years old, he joined Benfica's youth academy. Here he was assigned the position of midfielder, although this soon changed to center-back.

By 2015 his skills were ready for the professional league. He played for Benfica B in the 2015-2016 season, starting against the Chaves. He then caught a lucky break as he was asked to play in Benfica's UEFA Champions League round of 16. Three out of four of their usual center-backs couldn't go to Russia for the game.

His input was instrumental in the B team finishing fourth, the highest position it had ever recorded. By 2017 he played for the

Benfica first team and quickly showed anyone watching how good he was, including a stunning display against Manchester United.

By the end of the season, despite being out of action for a month due to appendicitis, he gained the title of best young player of the year.

Of course, the hard work he put into practicing and improving wasn't going unnoticed. Several of the biggest clubs in Europe were looking at him. In fact, there was a lot of speculation regarding a move to Lyon. Dias decided this wasn't for him and stayed at Benfica.

However, less than a year later, after a stunning opening goal against Moreirense, Benfica couldn't hold onto him anymore. Dias joined Manchester City for a staggering €68 million.

He played his first game for Manchester City on 3 October 2020 and helped them achieve a draw 1-1 against Leeds United.

But, it wasn't just his skills earning him praise. Despite his comparatively young age, Dias brought stability to the Manchester City team. His composure and leadership skills helped bring discipline to the squad. The result was, by the end of the 2020-2021 season, Manchester City had regained the Premier League title.

His performances and leadership by example earned him the Footballer of the Year award for the 2020-2021 season. It's notable that he was the first defender to win this award since Steve Nicol did in the 1988-1989 season.

The 2021-2022 season saw Dias named as captain for Manchester City. In his first game as captain, he provided the assist which allowed Jack Grealish to score, making it a 6-3 victory against RB Leipzig.

Dias was, unfortunately, hit with a hamstring injury in March 2022. It was the first injury he had experienced in five years of professional football. That's impressive.

The injury meant he was out of action for two months. He continued to build team morale from the sidelines and returned late in April to help Manchester City win 3-0 against Brighton & Hove Albion.

Unfortunately, a couple of weeks later he had a second hamstring injury which put him out of action for the rest of the season.

The good news was this left him fully fit for the 2022-2023 season. In fact, he managed to play almost every minute of every game for Manchester City during the 2022-2023 season! This included captaining the team to their first-ever Champions League win. They beat Inter Milan 1-0 in the Champions League final.

Perhaps what is most impressive about Dias's performance is that he immediately lowered the number of goals conceded by Manchester City, and yet also managed to initiate attacks with precision. It was almost like he knew where the opposition would be and could guide the ball around them.

His strong presence is what brings stability. However, it's his communication that ensures the team works well as one and suggests there is a bright future for Manchester City, for as long as they can hold onto his talent.

Dias's skills haven't been lost to Portugal. He joined the Under-17 side at the 2014 UEFA European Under-17 Championship. His performance earned him the captaincy for the under-19 Portuguese side at the 2016 UEFA European Under-19 Championship.

He also captained the U-20 side at the U-20 World Cup in 2017. The team made it to the quarterfinals before losing to Uruguay.

While his presence in the Portuguese team has yet to lead them to victory, he earned his 50th cap for the team in the UEFA Euro 2024 qualifiers against Luxembourg and guided the team to win 9-0. That's Portugal's biggest-ever international win and a positive sign of what is still to come from this talented player.

FUN FACTS ABOUT DIAS

- His jersey number at Manchester City and for the Portuguese team is number 3
- Dias has one older brother and two younger sisters
- His girlfriend, Marianna Goncalvez is a successful singer. Her stage name is April Ivy
- Dias scored his first Primeira Liga goal on 3 February 2018
- He has over 412,000 Instagram followers!

QUICK TRIVIA TEST

What's Dias's brother called?

Ivan

What nickname did his brother give Dias?

Ruby

What was the score in his debut match for Manchester City against Leeds United?

1-1

How much was his transfer fee to Manchester City?

€68 million

What injury did he have in March 2022?

Hamstring

FIVE LIFE LESSONS

1. Lead by example

Dias has been praised for his composure, leadership skills, and the stability he brings to his team. He achieves this by leading by example. Instead of preaching what his teammates should be doing, he simply does it.

That's something everyone can try to do.

2. Stay calm in any situation

One of the first things people note about this young player is that he retains his composure, regardless of what is going on around him.

It's this ability that helps him to see the right play to make and guide his team. It often results in victory and is a powerful reminder that staying calm works.

Next time you feel wound up, take a deep, breath and pause.

3. Play to win

Whether you're playing soccer, another game, or simply playing the game of life, play to win. Your attitude makes a big difference.

As Ruben says "I have watched the Premier League for ages and especially when I came, one thing that was in my mind is that whoever wins it, they deserve it. There is no chance of someone winning it that doesn't deserve it. You play against the best; you play to win."

Adopt that attitude in your own life.

4. Learn to relax

Stress can be useful to improve performance. However, too much stress is harmful to your health.

In short, you need to be able to relax and unwind for your own health. It's one thing that Dias admits he's not good at doing.

5. Be Open To Opportunities

A young Dias wanted to play as a striker. However, the team badly needed defenders and he switched. Ultimately, Dias has become one of the best center-backs in the world.

This was only possible because he was open to opportunities and supporting the team in any capacity. It led him to find his true soccer calling and allowed him to lead his team to victory over and over again.

All you have to do is be open to trying something different.

JOSE BOSINGWA
THE FLYING PORTUGUESE
WINGBACK

Jose Bosingwa was born in August 1982 and became one of the best right-backs in the world. He was born in Mbandaka, Zaire, (now known as the Democratic Republic of Congo) and the path to success wasn't always smooth.

His mother was Congolese and his father was Portuguese. It resulted in him moving to Portugal when he was just a few years old.

Although his father worked, Bosingwa was the youngest of ten children, that's a lot of mouths to feed! In short, as a child he was poor. Like many other children in his area, he spent most of his time outside.

Bosingwa quickly discovered that he had a passion for soccer. Better still, he was good at it. Even as a child, he had excellent ball control skills and he was fast. His pace frequently allowed him to outdistance older children.

He was enrolled in the local youth team, giving him a chance to practice, improve his skills, and make additional friends.

A scout from the local team, Freeamunde, watched him play and offered him a spot at the academy. He was just 12 when he started at the Freeamunde Academy. At the tender age of 15, he was offered a spot with the Boavista youth team.

He continued to play well and in 2000, when he had just turned 18, he was granted a spot on the senior team, officially starting his professional career.

This is where he encountered his first serious issue. The team had signed him as a defender but Bosingwa didn't have the brute strength needed to play in defense and hold back the attackers. This meant, while he trained with the first team, he wasn't selected for any games.

In effect, his career stalled before it even started.

Bosingwa didn't give up. He put all his effort into improving his skills and building additional muscle. Just a few months later it paid off, Bosingwa was offered an opportunity to play as a left-back. He quickly impressed on the field and started to appear in more games.

Unfortunately, he encountered several injuries during the season, limiting his ability to really shine.

In 2003, after two good seasons with Boavbista, Boswinga moved to Porto At the time it was coached by José Mourinho. As a newcomer and relative unknown, Boswinga wasn't used much during the first season at Porto. He played just 13 Liga games and 8 Champions League matches as Porto took the championship.

Mourinho departed and Bosingwa became Porto's first choice as right-back. It was the position he was born to play in and he was instrumental in leading the team to another three league victories.

It was during this period that he rolled his jeep down an embankment after driving too fast in wet conditions on the road. He and the other soccer players in his car survived. However, one of them needed to have their left foot amputated, marking the end of their career.

After such success with Porto, it wasn't a surprise to find some big clubs knocking at his door. Specifically, Chelsea was interested. Boswinga signed with them in 2008, for an impressive £13.6 million. He played his first game for Chelsea on 17 August 2008, one that they won 4-0. It was the start of a winning streak and several goals from Boswinga.

Despite several incidents on the field, his popularity grew and FC Bayern Munich tried to sign Boswinga in 2009. He stayed at Chelsea and then incurred a knee injury which knocked him out of action for the rest of the season.

It was a stressful year, dedicated to rehabilitation, Boswinga didn't play for Chelsea again until October 2010. He was effectively unable to play for a year! He played sporadically for the season. However, when he was allowed to play as right back, his natural position, he again shone.

He was vital to Chelsea's successful efforts to win the Champions League against FC Bayern Munich, they were the first London club to achieve this.

Despite the strength of the Chelsea back four, Boswinga's contract was not renewed. He switched to Queens Park Rangers and played with them for just three months.

It was a tough time for Boswinga. He scored an impressive goal in his first game with QPR, firing the ball into the back of the net from close range. There were just six minutes of play left.

Unfortunately, QPR were still relegated that season and Boswinga was seen smiling about it. He left QPR after three months and moved to Trabzonspor in the Turkish Super Lig, finishing his career by bringing new attention to Turkey as a soccer nation.

Of course, such talent wasn't wasted on Portugal. Boswinga had acquired naturalization as a child and was eligible for the national team. He first played for them in May 2007, helping them to win 2-1 against Belgium in the UEFA Euro 2008 qualifiers.

His performance ensured he became the first choice for the team, he played in all the matches and helped Portugal get to the quarter-finals. Impressively, he was part of the team of the tournament.

FUN FACTS ABOUT BOSINGWA

- He won 15 major titles while at Chelsea and Porto
- Arriving at Chelsea he was given the number 16 jersey but switched for number 17 with Scott Sinclair
- In October 2009 he injured his knee and was out of action for a year
- He scored a total of six goals in his club career, not bad for a right-back!
- Bosingwa has nine brothers and sisters

QUICK TRIVIA TEST

When was Bosingwa born?

1982

At what age did he sign up to the Freeamunde Academy

12

How long was he unable to play after his knee injury?

One year

When did he first play for Portugal?

May 2007

What team did he finish his career with?

Trabzonspor in the Turkish Super Lig

FIVE LIFE LESSONS

1. Give It Your All

Bosingwa could have become downhearted, reduced his training, or even given up when he was deemed too small to play defense for Boavista.

Instead, he showed why it's worthwhile to give something your all. He improved physically and mentally so that when he got an opportunity, he impressed. That ensured his future success.

2. Think of others

Bosingwa crashed his jeep. It was an accident but his speed contributed to it. The result was that one of the soccer players in the car, Sandro Luis, had his foot amputated, effectively ending his career.

Accidents happen, but being aware of the situation around you and the people you're with may have prevented this one. It's important to think about others and potential consequences.

3. Never be afraid to apologize

Everyone says things in the heat of the moment that they wish they hadn't. A perfect example of this is when Bosingwa said about the referee in the 2009 Champions League semifinal "I don't know whether he's a referee or a thief."

He later apologized, proving that you should own your actions and never be afraid to apologize.

4. Do your job

No matter what role you have do your job and do it well. If you focus on that everything else will fall into place. This is certainly true for Bosingwa, he played well at Chelsea, despite injuries. Many people today feel that it was Bosingwa who was the real mastermind behind Chelse's Champions League win.

He achieved this by not focusing on the glory, but simply on the task at hand.

5. Modesty keeps you grounded

When you are good at something it's easy to feel you are better than others. However, this is a slippery slope which often leads to making mistakes and alienating people.

Remember, you're simply part of a team. That's why Bosingwa chose parts of lots of different players when selecting his perfect player. None of them were him.

Recognizing your good is important, but you don't need to think you're better than anyone else. A little humility goes a long way.

VIRGIL VAN DIJK
A LATE GROWER

Virgil Van Dijk is known as a center-back and as the captain of Liverpool and the Netherlands national team. He's an exceptionally talented player, recognized by many people as one of the best defenders of his generation.

Today, he is also known for his leadership qualities, his speed on the field, and his ability to handle the ball in the air.

Of course, he hasn't always been a high-earning celebrity soccer player!

Van Dijk was born in July 1991 in Breda, the Netherlands. His father was Dutch and his mother Afro-Surinamese. He's the oldest of three children. His father left when he was just 11 years old.

Van Dijk chose to live with his father. However, after a short time, he returned to his mother and lost contact with his father.

His childhood was fairly standard, a product of separated parents, he played football whenever and wherever he could. It led to him joining the youth team at the age of eight.

At that stage, he was simply a member of the Willem II Academy. Without a contract. As a teenager, he started earning money as a dishwasher, it was a conscious decision to help out at home and start building skills for the future. Of course, he hoped playing soccer would lead somewhere.

Perhaps the biggest change happened when he turned 17. Until that point, Van Dijk had been fairly short and played as a right-back. He didn't excel in this position. However, when he turned 17 he grew 18 cm almost overnight! It allowed him to be moved into a central defensive position.

His game instantly improved, but the academy felt he wasn't good enough for the first team and didn't offer him a contract.

Undeterred, he took a free transfer to FC Groningen. It was 2010 and he had just turned 19. It wasn't until 1 May 2011 that he got to play for Groningen, the staff felt he had been overworked at the academy and needed a break.

His first game experience with Groningen started in the 72nd minute when he was substituted for Petter Andersson. His first starting match with the team was at the end of May and he scored his first goal, helping the team to win 5-1.

Just as Van Dijk was starting to regularly star in the first team, he faced a new issue. He had barely turned 20 when he was sent to hospital for advanced appendicitis, peritonitis, and kidney poisoning. After an urgent operation, he spent a further 13 days in the hospital and wasn't allowed to walk for another 10 days. He also lost two and a half stone.

It knocked him out of games for several months but he committed to rehabilitation and training, rebuilding his strength. He returned in the summer of 2012 and, alongside Kees Kwakman, created a formidable defensive team.

2013 saw him bartering with several clubs but not securing a suitable transfer. However, near the end of June, he managed to sign a deal with Celtic. His debut with Celtic happened on 17th August, he came on for the final 13 minutes.

Celtic could see his talent and he became a regular. Perhaps one of his most memorable performances was the solo run against St Johnstone on 26 December. He scored and secured Celtic's victory 1-0!

There were a surprising number of goals from Van Dijk that season, Celtic won the League and Van Dijk was nominated for the PFA Scotland's Player of the Year award and was included in the PFA Scotland Team of the Year.

In short, his talent was finally being recognized. The following season, his performance and playtime increased. He scored the opening goal in a 4-0 win over Motherwell and the final goal in the match against Dundee United, setting up a Cup final replay.

Unfortunately, through no fault of Van Dijk, Celtic failed to win the Scottish League Cup for the third time.

Van Dijk's journey wasn't over. On the last day of the 2015 transfer window, he signed with Southampton, a club in the English Premier League. The transfer fee was £13 million, making it the most expensive for a Dutch defender since Jaap Stam.

The 2015-2016 season was excellent, Van Dijk was named Player of the Year by the fans and his teammates, which led to him becoming the team captain in 2017. His performance led to interest from several of the top Premier League clubs, the following season he transferred to Liverpool. The fee was an impressive £75 million!

He showed Liverpool he was worth the money by scoring in his first appearance for the team, something that hadn't been done at Southampton since 1901!

His skill and performance were credited with the sudden strength in Liverpool's defense, which had previously been struggling.

Van Dijk appeared in roughly half of Liverpool's games in the first season. His next season was infinitely better. He won Player of the Month in August and the Premier League Player of the Month in December. He was also nominated for the PFA Players' Player of the Year and was included in the PFA Team of the Year.

In addition, Van Dijk was runner-up for the Best FIFA Men's Player and made it into the FIFA FIFpro Men's World 11! He was even shortlisted for the Ballon d'Or.

Van Dijk missed much of the 2020-2021 season due to a torn ACVL and subsequent surgery/rehabilitation. However, when he returned in July 2021 it was clear he hadn't lost any of his talent. He became Liverpool's team captain in July 2023.

Van Dijk has also played for the Netherlands national team. He first played in the U19 squad, then the U21. However, his first appearance in the senior team was in 2014, although he didn't play on the field until October 2015!

In March 2018 he was made captain of the Netherlands national team and inspired his teammates. That was the year they made it to the Nations League final, losing to Portugal 1-0.

He repeated his inspirational leadership by taking the Netherlands to the quarter-finals in the 2022 FIFA World Cup, losing on penalties to Argentina.

FUN FACTS ABOUT VAN DIJK

- Van Dijk is a right-footed center-back capable of playing on the right or left of center
- When he was a child he was a huge fan of Barcelona
- He is heavily involved in charity and is the ambassador for an orphanage in Nepal
- Van Dijk is the only defender to win UEFA Men's Player of the Year
- He was named Premier League Player of the Season and PFA Players' Player of the Year in his first season with Celtic

QUICK TRIVIA TEST

When was Van Dijk born?

July 1991

How many brothers and sisters does Van Dijk have?

Two

How much did Van Dijk grow when he turned 17?

An impressive 18cm!

When did he become the Liverpool captain?

July 2023

When did he become captain of the Netherlands national team?

March 2018

FIVE LIFE LESSONS

1. Keep your options open

Van Dijk was confident that he would make it as a soccer player. However, he didn't rely completely on his skill. Instead, he started working and earning money, building his skillset for the future.

It turns out he didn't need to, but it's always a good idea to keep as many options open as possible.

2. Keep trying whatever happens

There will be setbacks in life, particularly times when people tell you that you can't do something.

These are the times when you need to try the hardest, not to prove yourself to others but to be the best you can be, for yourself.

Van Dijk did this when Willem II Academy felt he wasn't good enough for the first team. He never stopped trying and ultimately succeeded.

3. Be Confident

Van Dijk's Celtic teammate once said, "He had an aura about him, a confidence because I think he knew he was good."

Being confident in your own abilities is a good thing, as long as you accept help from others and don't become arrogant about your abilities.

4. Recognize those that help you

Van Dijk is married to Rike Nooitgedagt. She was a successful fashion sales manager but had to quit to stay with Van Dijk when he transferred to Celtic. She chose to give up her career to support her husband, he recognizes this sacrifice and often pays tribute to her.

You should do the same for those who sacrifice for you.

5. Don't stick to one thing

Van Dijk is a defender and a very good one. However, he's also a versatile player and has been required to play as a striker on several occasions. That's helped him score goals and compete with other strikers.

It's a rare ability in modern football and a reminder that you shouldn't stay in your comfort zone, always accept new challenges.

I have included these free downloadable gifts to help light up your inner inspiration & reach your potential.

While you are reading through the stories, lessons and trivia, we recommend that you make use of all the bonuses we've attached here!

All our bonuses have been made specifically to help young athletes feel fired up, get inspired from the best to ever do it, and most importantly fall more in love with this incredible game!

Here's a list of what you're getting-

1) 250 Fun Facts From The World Of Sports
2) Sports Practice and Game Calendar
3) 5 Fun Exercise Drills for Kids
4) The BEST Advice From The Greatest Athletes Of All Time
5) The Mental Mindset Guided Meditation & Affirmation Collection
6) The Most Famous Events In Sports History And What They Can Teach Us

Now, it's over to you to scan the QR code, follow the instructions & get started!

RICARDO BOAVISTA'S CHAMPION

Ricardo's full name is Ricardo Alexandre Martins Soares Pereira, but he is simply known as Ricardo. He's now retired but is potentially one of the best goalkeepers to have ever graced the game.

Ricardo was born in 1976 in Montijo, Setubal, there was nothing particularly remarkable about his childhood. He had both parents and they tried to give him the best possible start in life.

Like many children of the period, he spent most of his free time outdoors. Specifically, he was passionate about playing football. He practiced with his friends daily, each egging the other on.

It was around this time that Ricardo discovered he was good at saving the ball, making him an automatic choice as goalkeeper. It certainly made it easier for his friends as most of them didn't want to take turns in the goal.

His skills and dedication were noticed by his parents. They enlisted him in the local youth team, Unidos Barreiro. Ricardo was just 11 years old when he started with them, and 14 when he moved on.

During his time at Unidos, he quickly confirmed his calling as a goalkeeper. Ricardo earned a name for himself as a first-class keeper.

This led to interest from other teams and in 1990, the young Ricardo signed with Montijo, the soccer club based in his hometown.

He continued to flourish for another year in the youth team before being transferred to the senior team for a year. During that year he played in 18 games. By the end of the 1994-1995 season, he was approached by Boavista with an offer he simply couldn't refuse.

Although he had already garnered a good reputation, as soon as he arrived at Boavista, Ricardo found himself battling with William Andem, they were both goalkeepers and both chasing the number one spot.

Fortunately for Ricardo, he found himself better and subsequently earned the first-choice position. It allowed him to play in games between 1995 and 2003. This included being in 28 of the Primeira Liga Championship matches, a championship they ultimately won. It was, and still is, the only club title the club has ever earned.

His performance in the 2002-2003 UEFA Cup was particularly noteworthy. He was instrumental in the team making it as far as the semi-finals, an impressive achievement.

He even managed to score a penalty kick in May 2003, effectively giving his team the win against S.C. Beira-Mar.

Ricardo was still warming up! As the next season started it was revealed that Ricardo had transferred to Sporting CP. The fee was an impressive €7 million.

With such a good reputation, Ricardo had no problem being picked as first-choice keeper for every game. He was instrumental in Sporting's progression in the UEFA Cup. They made it to the final where they lost 3-1 to PFC CSKA Moscow.

Ricardo stayed with the team until 2007 when he transferred to Real Betis. This was a tougher period for him on the field. He started with Real Betis as the number-one keeper. However, due to poor performance, the trainee Casto, took over.

Fortunately, Ricardo returned to form and became the first-choice again at the end of the season. It was the start of several years where he spent more time on the bench than on the field. Potentially a disappointing end to the star's career.

However, he was inspired by Sven-Goran Eriksson and made the move to Leicester City. Once again, Ricardo found his form and he enjoyed an excellent season with the team. However, at this stage, Ricardo was 37 years old and past his soccer prime.

He chose to return to his home country and played for another two years with S.C. Olhanense. It proved to be the perfect way to wind down his career while still giving some of the best performances of his life.

Of course, with such skills, it was inevitable that Ricardo would be picked for the Portuguese national team. He played his first match for them in 2001, replacing the injured Vitor Baia.

It was during his time with the Portugal national team that he made one of the most famous, perhaps iconic, saves the game has ever seen. It cemented his place as one of the greats.

The scene was Euro 2004, it was a disappointing tournament for many teams, especially the biggest ones like Italy, Spain, and Germany: they were all knocked out at the group, stages.

Portugal had faired better and made it to the quarterfinals, setting up a match against England. Michael Own scored in the first three minutes, sipping a goal past Ricardo. England stayed ahead until an eightieth-minute goal from Helder Postiga.

Extra time produced extra goals but the score remained even, taking it to penalty shootouts. Even these were level-pegged, both teams scored four of them, leaving the match to go to sudden death.

Ricardo knew the players, who had studied their form and where they liked to shoot. But, for the sudden death he was presented with Darius Vassell, he had never seen him shoot a penalty.

Ricardo still doesn't know why he did it, but he tore off his gloves and waited. Vassell was nervous and Ricardo believed he could save it. He dived left as the shot came, blocking it with his barehand. A moment later, Ricardo took his turn, blasting his penalty shot past the England keeper and sealing the win for Portugal.

It was perhaps one of the most memorable pieces of Portuguese soccer of all time.

FUN FACTS ABOUT RICARDO

- Despite being the goalkeeper, Ricardo scored one goal with Boavista.
- He played in 369 league games and 62 European Cup games.
- Ricardo played for Portugal 79 times, including playing in two World Cups.
- Despite being a goalkeeper, Ricardo never had a serious injury while on the field.
- Ricardo was given the Medal of Merit, effectively a Portuguese knighthood, after his performance at Euro 2004.

QUICK TRIVIA TEST

What's Ricardo's full name?

Ricardo Alexandre Martins Soares Pereira

When was Ricardo born?

1976

How old was Ricardo when he started with Unidos Barreiro?

Eleven

What was the transfer fee paid by Sporting CP?

€7 million

Whose penalty did Ricardo save without a glove?

Darius Vassell

FIVE LIFE LESSONS

1. Do what you do best

A little variation is good for people, it prevents you from stagnating. It's good to reach outside your comfort zone occasionally.

However, that doesn't mean you have to take change just for the sake of change. Ricardo stayed with two clubs during the peak of his career. He turned down offers and avoided the England Premier League because he was happy where he was.

Sometimes, it's simply better to do what you do best without changing it.

2. Don't take anything for granted

When you're good at something it's easy to take that skill for granted. However, if you do that you are likely to lose your edge.

It's important to practice and improve all your skills, you never know when you'll need them professionally or otherwise.

3. Know when to quit

Ricardo had an excellent career as a goalkeeper and made several memorable saves. However, he knew when his career was winding down and chose to leave the spotlight while still in good form.

Sometimes, it's good to know when to quit and start something new.

4. Competition is healthy

Several times in Ricardo's career he had to fight for the first place in his team. It's not surprising, competition is generally tough for all the spots on a professional football team.

Ricardo prevailed on most occasions but the simple act of competing is what really matters. It brings out a healthy instinct to be the best you can be.

5. Believe in yourself

When Vassell stepped up to take the penalty for England, Ricardo had already allowed in two goals during the game and four in penalties. He could have simply given up.

Instead, he believed he could save the penalty and score his own penalty kick. It was his belief that allowed him to do this, not the symbolic gesture of removing his gloves.

You should also believe in what you can do

PETER SCHMEICHEL
A CLEAN SHEET LEGEND

Peter Boleslaw Schmeichel is one of the best goalies to ever play in the English Premier League and potentially one of the greatest goalies ever. He was born in Gladsaxe, a small suburb of Copenhagen in Denmark. The year was 1963 when Inger and Antoni welcomed baby Peter to the family.

With three sisters, Schmeichel was the only boy in the family, but that didn't stop him from being close to his siblings or from playing soccer on the local streets. Perhaps it was his instinct to defend his sisters that made him gravitate towards the goal. Whatever the reason, it was quickly clear that the young Schmeichel had talent.

His parents signed him up with the local youth team, he was just eight years old. At the time, he didn't know where this journey would take him. However, after two and a half years with his local Gladsaxe team, he started drawing a lot of attention. After all, at that stage, he had gone two and a half years without letting a goal in!

It was BK Hero who approached him first, he seized the opportunity and continued to hone his skills.

During his time there he achieved several seemingly impossible tasks. Of particular merit was his play against Stubbekobing. His keeping skills helped Hero win the game and prevented them from being relegated.

Of course, during this time Schmeichel didn't have a contract. This included working in a dyeing department of a textile factory and as a cleaner at an old people's home. He worked a variety of jobs before being offered a professional contract by Brondby in 1987.

Brondby was in good shape, they had been runners-up in the league the year before Schmeichel signed with them. He played with them for four seasons and was instrumental in them winning the league for those four seasons.

In 1991 he helped Brondy reach the semi-finals of the UEFA Cup. He even managed a clean sheet in several of the matches. It resulted in Schmeichel being voted 10th in the IFFHS World's Best Goalkeeper.

At this stage, Schmeichel was 27 years old, but he had a lot left to give the sport. On 6th August 1991 Manchester United signed Schmeichel for £505,000. The club considered it an absolute bargain because there was little awareness of Schmeichel outside of Denmark.

It was the break Schmeichel needed to excel. In the first season with Manchester United, they were runners-up in the league, won the Football League Cup, and Schmeichel was named the IFFHS World's Best Goalkeeper. He jumped ten places in just one season!

The following season Schmeichel delivered 22 clean sheet games, resulting in Manchester United winning the Premier League for the first time in 26 years. Again, he was voted the World's Best Goalkeeper.

Schmeichel appeared in 292 games for Manchester United with many of them having clean sheets. Perhaps the highlight of his time with United was at the end. His final season with the club resulted in them winning all three cups, the Premier League, FA Cup, and the UEFA Champions League.

It was the season where Schmeichel made a stunning save as Dennis Bergkamp took a penalty in the last few minutes of the FA Cup semi-final. A save that drove the game into extra time and another win for United.

For the UEFA Champions League final, United were missing captain Roy Keane. Schmeichel took the captaincy and, near the end of the game, took the unusual decision to run toward the oppositions goal as United took a corner. The confusion helped Sheringham score an equalizer. The subsequent revival of United saw Ole Gunner Solskjaer score the winner just a few moments later, giving United a 2-1 victory and the UEFA Champions League Cup.

Schmeichel was 36 when he left United, a mutual leaving based on Schmeichel being concerned with his ability to maintain a high standard over a 60-game season. He moved to Sporting CP in Portugal and helped them win the Primeira Liga title in his first season with them.

The second season didn't go as well, with his contract up, Schmeichel moved to Aston Villa and back to the English Premier League. It was while playing with Aston Villa that he became the first goalkeeper to score a Premier League goal!

The following season he transferred to Manchester City, a shock to his old Manchester United fans. In a testimony to his skill, even approaching 40, he ensured Manchester City never lost to Manchester United. He had done the same feat for United when playing City!

That impressive feat ensured that potentially the best goalkeeper on the planet retired at the top of his game.

Naturally, Schmeichel also played for the Denmark national team. His first appearance in the national squad was in 1987. He became the starting keeper in the UEFA Euro 1988. Denmark didn't perform well but the experience helped shape the young Schmeichel.

It was a different story in Euro 1992 when Schmeichel was instrumental in Denmark winning the tournament. Despite many international games with clean sheets for Schmeichel, Euro 1992 was the best performance from Denmark, and one that will not soon be forgotten.

FUN FACTS ABOUT PETER SCHMEICHEL

- Schmeichel is 6ft 4in tall, weighs close to 16 stone and needed specially made XXXL soccer shirts.
- He has been capped 129 times for the Denmark national team, more than any other player.
- Schmeichel has the record for the most clean sheets in the Premier League.
- He won an impressive five Premier League titles while at Manchester United.
- Schmeichel was inducted into the English Football Hall of Fame in 2003.

QUICK TRIVIA TEST

What's Schmeichel's full name?

Peter Boleslaw Schmeichel

What age was Schmeichel when he joined his first team?

Eight

What year did he get his first professional contract?

1987

What year did he first win the IFFHS World's Best Goalkeeper award?

1992

What was he the first goalkeeper in the Premier League to do?

Score a goal

FIVE LIFE LESSONS

1. Hard work pays off

Schmeichel worked multiple jobs to earn money while trying to win a professional soccer contract. It was hard work balancing work, training, and matches. However, he was committed and eventually got the contract he deserved.

As he said, "Hard work beats talent when talent doesn't work hard."

2. Believe in yourself

Schmeichel is quoted as saying "You have to believe in yourself to win." It's something he believed was true and something you should apply to your daily life.

If you believe you can do it, you can.

3. Learn from your mistakes

Schmeichel wasn't a perfect goalie, he made mistakes, let goals in, and even made some poor decisions. In short, he is human!

But, as he says, "Don't dwell on mistakes, learn from them and move on." That's an important mindset for anyone to have.

4. It's impossible to control the future

Schmeichel once said, "You can't control what happens to you, but you can control how you react to it."

It's true, you can't tell what is going to happen next. However, by learning to pause before you react and choosing your reaction, you can get the best out of any situation. It's a mantra he lived by.

5. Put Others First

Schmeichel may have been the first goalkeeper to score a Premier League goal, but that wasn't his intent when captaining

United in the UEFA Champions League Cup. He simply ran forward to distract the opposition, allowing his teammates to score.

It was a great example of putting others first and of thinking fast. Skills which are useful in daily life.

JORDAN HENDERSON
THE WHITE YAYA TOURÈ

Jordan Brian Henderson was born on 17 June 1990 and is a well-established and versatile midfielder. He's known for his leadership qualities and has proved to be an asset for several clubs over the years.

As with so many soccer players, he discovered a passion for the game when young. It's a passion that has never left him and is instrumental to his success.

He was born in Tyne and Wear, Sunderland, England. His parent were normal people, a fitness teacher and a police officer.

From a young age, he kicked the ball around with his dad and his friends, the family were ardent Sunderland supporters and supported Henderson's decision to join the Sunderland Academy when he was just eight years old.

It was the right decision. After a decade of honing his skills, he joined the Sunderland first team. His first match as a professional was in November 2008. The team lost 5-0 to Chelsea.

The following season he was loaned to Coventry City. It started as a one-month loan but they requested he stay. It was a valuable learning experience for him and led to his first goal in a game against Norwich City.

Unfortunately, late in the season, he fractured the fifth metatarsal in his foot, putting him out of action for the rest of the season. Henderson returned to Sunderland for the 2009 season.

It was immediately apparent that his time at Coventry City had helped his skill on the field. He appeared in 38 matches for Sunderland and even scored twice. Notably, his first Premier League goal was against Manchester City.

His designated position was right midfield. However, the season also saw him demonstrate his versatility. When Lee Cattermole was out of action, Henderson moved to the center and played just as well.

It helped him earn the Sunderland Young Player of the Year award.

The following season saw him appear 39 times and score three goals. His skills were certainly noticed, Liverpool bid somewhere between £15 and $20 million for the player and he started with Liverpool in the first game of the season. Funnily, it was against Sunderland, the club he had just left. The Sunderland fans gave him a mixed reception.

This was to be his home for the next decade. Henderson became a stabilizing force in the team and a valuable asset.

In his first season with Liverpool, he played in 48 games and scored twice. The following season saw him score his first European goal and the goal that allowed Liverpool to qualify for the UEFA Europa League.

It wasn't until the 2013-2014 season that he was considered a regular member of the squad, appearing in nearly every match. Unfortunately, a sliding tackle against Manchester City resulted in a three-match ban meant Liverpool finished second in the league, instead of first.

While Henderson missed much of the 2015-2016 with injury, it was also the year he was officially made captain. Out of just 26 appearances, he scored two goals.

It didn't stop him coming back string in 2016-2017. Of particular note was his goal against Chelsea, a match Liverpool won. Henderson scored with an impressive kick from 25 yards out. It won the award for Premiership Goal of the Month.

As Liverpool captain, he also led the team right up to the Champions League final. Unfortunately, they finished as runner-sup when Real Madrid beat them 3-1. It was a feat that the team managed again the following season. Henderson even played through a knee injury to get them there. This time, they beat Barcelona 4-0, overcoming a 3-0 deficit. It's considered one of the best comebacks in the history of the Champions League.

Henderson went on to captain the squad in the final, winning 2-0 over Tottenham Hotspur to lift the UEFA Champions League trophy. They went on to beat Chelsea on penalties and take the 2019 UEFA Super Cup and their first FIFA Club World Cup title.

In short, Henderson guided and was instrumental in Liverpool collecting all three continental trophies, something that no other English club has done.

It's worth noting that, despite being a midfielder, Henderson has scored 22 times for Liverpool. The majority of these have been impressive goals from long distance, reminding everyone how powerful and versatile this player is.

The treble was impressive, but Henderson wasn't done. Although Covid-19 caused a break in soccer, play resumed after and, on 25 June 2020, Henderson captained Liverpool to win the Premier League, the first time they had achieved this in 30 years!

As a result, he was named FWA Footballer of the Year and was a finalist for PFA Player's Player of the Year.

In 2021, at the age of 31, Henderson signed a new contract with Liverpool. The same year Liverpool beat Manchester United at

Old Trafford 5-0. The most memorable goal of a fantastic game was from Salah, he received a dream pass from Henderson which completely split the defense.

This was the year he reached 300 appearances for Liverpool.

If possible, 2022 was even better. Henderson steered Liverpool to win the 2021-2022 FA Cup and the EFL Cup. The team just missed out on winning the Premier League and the UEFA Champions League. It would have been a historic quadruple and a fitting end to his time at Liverpool.

FUN FACTS ABOUT JORDAN HENDERSON

- He has been a Sunderland fan from the moment he was born
- Henderson's biggest motivation is his father and the strength he displayed fighting cancer
- Jordan Henderson wears Nike shoes on the field because he's sponsored by them
- He's married with two daughters and one son
- During the Covid-19 pandemic he helped raise millions of pounds for the NHS

QUICK TRIVIA TEST

At what age did he join Sunderland Academy?

Aged Eight

What year did he make his Sunderland first-team debut?

2008

Who did he score his first professional goal against?

Norwich City

How many times did he play in his first full season with Sunderland?

38

Which year did Henderson achieve 300 appearances for Liverpool?

2021

FIVE LIFE LESSONS

1. Keep it clean

Henderson performed a dangerous sliding tackle against Samir Nasri when playing against Manchester City. The result was his first red card and a three-match ban.

Liverpool lost two of those matches and drew the other, giving up the top spot in the league to Manchester City. It ultimately cost them the league. Although no one can know what would have happened if Henderson had been on the field for those three games, keeping it clean may have made a big difference to Liverpool that season.

2. Go the distance

In the modern world, it has become common to switch between roles, jobs, and even partners. Henderson decided not to go for this route, instead dedicating himself to one team: Liverpool.

The result was he built an unbeatable rapport with his teammates and led them to a historic number of victories.

Sometimes, it's worth sticking with what you know.

3. Always look to improve yourself

Henderson didn't have the best start at Liverpool. It took him two years to be considered a regular. He believes that his hunger to improve himself is the main reason he improved and became such an unstoppable force

That drive to improve himself is still present today and is something everyone should try to emulate.

4. Strive to be a role model

This simply involves pausing and thinking about what is best for the club, the game, or whatever you are involved in. It's something that Henderson has learnt to do and makes every situation better for him and those around him.

As he says, "We all have the same goal – and that's to bring success to this club and our incredible supporters."

5. Don't worry about what others say

It's human nature to need a scapegoat, someone to blame when it all goes wrong. At many times in his career, that scapegoat has been Henderson. He doesn't let it affect him negatively.

Instead, as he says "With the criticism and the negative things, I always think that makes me better."

In short, use the blame to make yourself a better person.

CARLOS BOCANEGRA
THE JACKAL

Carlos Bocanegra has won the MLS Defender of the Year title twice. He's a well-recognized defender who has played in England, Scotland, Spain, and even France, with some of the best soccer teams in the world.

He was born in Upland, a city in San Bernardino County, California. The city is close to Los Angeles County. It has a good reputation and is considered a desirable place to live. But that didn't mean Bocanegra wanted to stay there forever.

He was born in May 1979 and went to Alta Loma High School with his brother Diego. Interestingly, Diego went on to play soccer at Grand Canyon University, UCLA, and Fresno State. He then went on to become head coach at the University of Houston, specifically looking after the women's soccer team.

Bocanegra also attended UCLA, studying history and geography.

He was always athletic and, before he chose UCLA, he was offered several scholarships with American Football. However, as soccer was his main goal he turned down the scholarships. Instead, he joined the UCLA Bruins while at UCLA.

It was enough to get him noticed and, upon finishing UCLA, he was offered a contract with Chicago Fire. He was, impressively, the fourth overall pick in the 2000 MLS SuperDraft. The majority of the season was played with the Chicago Fire, although he was loaned to Project-40 for two games.

Bocanegra helped the team make it to the MLS Championship and win the Lamar Hunt US Open Cup. He received the award for Rookie of the Year as recognition for his contribution.

In his four years in MLS, he scored five goals and assisted with eight others. Not bad for a defender.

His talent hadn't gone unnoticed across the pond. Fulham, a team in the English Premier League, signed him in January 2004. He mainly played as a center back, although, when needed, he played left back. For a short time, he even played holding midfielder.

His personality and skills instantly made him a hit with the fans. They nicknamed him the Jackal, some fans referred to him as the Black Snake.

It's easy to see why he was so popular, he attacked like a jackal and, despite playing as a left-back, he managed to score five goals during the 2006-2007 Premier League season. It made him the second-leading scorer for Fulham.

Bocanegra was a regular in the team, by 2007 he had played in 100 games.

The following year Bocanegra transferred to Rennes. Interestingly, he was given the number three short which is the same number he had in the US.

He performed well for Rennes, starting in 38 games throughout the season and scoring several times. Again, his performance didn't go unnoticed. In 2010 he transferred to Ligue 1 club Saint-Etienne, again being given the number three shirt.

Regular appearances throughout the next couple of seasons ensured that his play got even better, although the team struggled in the league. Bocanegra was injured in October 2010. A whiplash injury which occurred on the field stopped him from playing for three weeks.

In his last season with the club, he temporarily became captain and in 2011 he transferred to Rangers. He was instantly thrown into the thick of it, playing in the UEFA Europa League qualifier against Maribor. He even scored!

The Maribor team even complained to UEFA that he hadn't completed the required paperwork. The claim was rejected but Rangers never made it to the UEFA Europa League.

Unfortunately, the Rangers experienced financial trouble and, ultimately, Bocanegra went to Santander on a loan deal. He returned to Rangers a year later, but shortly after, signed for Chivas, a USA-based soccer team.

He played two good seasons with the club before retiring in 2014.

During this time, Bocanegra was also selected for the US national soccer team. He first played for them in the junior squad at the 199 FIFA World Youth Championship. In 2001 he played his official first senior game and quickly became a mainstay of the team.

In 2003 he appeared 13 times for the US national team, more than any other defender.

Unfortunately, the management couldn't decide his position for the World Cup Qualifier in 2005. He was moved back and forth between center back and left back. It didn't help him play better.

However, in 2007, Bocanegra was named captain of the US squad. His first outing as captain resulted in a 4-1 victory for the US against China. He also led the US to defeat Spain and win the 2009 FIFA Confederations Cup semi-finals.

Ultimately, he was capped for the US over 100 times. An impressive achievement for someone offered an American football sponsorship.

It's worth noting, that since retiring, Bocanegra has continued to give back to the beautiful game. He became the technical director for Atlanta United in March 2015 and has also been appointed to co-chair the Technical Development Committee at US Soccer.

FUN FACTS ABOUT BOCANEGRA

- While playing for UCLA he was named PAC-10 Player of the Year
- He has one brother who also played soccer
- Bocanegra was the first American player to captain a French Ligue 1 team!
- He earned a reputation for sportsmanship and fair play
- Bocanegra was inducted into the National Soccer Hall of Fame in 2020

QUICK TRIVIA TEST

Where was Bocanegra born

Upland, California

What year did Fulham sign Bocanegra?

2004

Which year did Bocanegra reach 100 appearances for Fulham?

2007

What year did Bocanegra retire?

2014

When did he first play for the US national soccer team?

1999

FIVE LIFE LESSONS

1. Stay true to what you believe in

Bocanegra was offered several American Football scholarships but turned them down as he was focused on soccer. This was risky as he may not have made it as a soccer player.

However, he chose to stay true to his own beliefs. It paid off in the end as he became a great soccer player and was inducted into the UCLA Athletics Hall of Fame in 2013.

2. Give it your all

Bocanegra earned the nickname "The Jackal" at Fulham. It's because he is completely committed to every attack.

Whether he liked the nickname or not, it was apt. Bocanegra is committed to giving his all in every situation. It's what has made him a talented soccer player.

3. Play Fair

Bocanegra earned a reputation for good sportsmanship and as a fair player. It's an attitude that served him well and has helped him secure valuable work post-soccer.

While soccer is a competition, there is no reason to be disrespectful to the other players. It's an attitude that works well in all walks of life.

4. Think of others

Bocanegra admits that Ranger's financial problems were a horrible time for him, it was a period of massive uncertainty. However, even during this period he urged the players to think of others and encouraged them to light up the dejected fans.

It helped them want him back when Rangers were solvent again, proving looking out for others isn't just the right thing to do, it can be beneficial.

5. Remember who you are

Bocanegra once said, "Never forget where you're from". It's true, even in the high-stakes world of professional soccer, you need to stay true to your own values.

There is no better way of doing that than by remembering where you're from.

NADINE ANGERER
A PENALTY SAVER OF THE
HIGHEST ORDER!

Nadine Angerer was born in November 1978 in Lohr am Main, a small town near Frankfurt, Germany. Today, she is seen as Germany's number-one female soccer player. She's achieved an impressive amount in a career on the field spanning three decades!

In fact, Angerer has developed a reputation as being an expert goalkeeper, particularly when faced with penalties.

Unlike many of the soccer stars on this list, Angerer wasn't obsessed with soccer as a young child. She indulged in an array of activities and only discovered soccer as a passion around her eighth birthday.

She appeared to have some talent and joined the local youth team, ASV Hofstetten, in her early teens. As she displayed good ball control, she was selected as a forward and played well for them.

However, her true calling was revealed a few years later. In 1994, when she was 16 years old, the goalkeeper at ASV Hofstetten was injured. She volunteered to take her place.

Even without goalkeeper training, her skills were instantly obvious. It was also fortuitous for her that several scouts were present at the game. After some discussions, she moved to FC Numberg in 1995, she was 17 and eligible for their senior squad.

A year later, as she honed her skills, she transferred to FC Wacker Munchen. It was around this time she was offered an opportunity to play for an American college soccer team. She chose not to accept the offer, preferring to focus on her career in Germany. She stayed at Wacker for four seasons before transferring to Bayern Munich in 1999.

Although only with Munich for two seasons, her goalkeeping skills were instrumental in the team being promoted, allowing them to enter the top division in Germany.

It promoted more interest from other clubs and, in 2001 she transferred to FFC Turbine Potsdam. It was here that her trophy collection really started to grow.

She played with the team for six seasons and helped them win the Bundesliga twice. She was also instrumental in the team winning the German Cup three times and, perhaps one of her greatest achievements, the UEFA Women's Cup in 2004-2005.

It's worth noting that she won the German Cup again with Frankfurt in 2011.

Angerer took a year out from German soccer to play for the Swedish team Djurgardens IF Dam. However, she missed the challenging environment of the Bundesliga and returned in 2009 to play with Frankfurt. She even became the captain at Frankfurt after Birgit Prinz retired.

However, some of her most famous and best saves happened on the international stage. She first featured in the German national team in 1996. However, for the best part of a decade, she played second fiddle to Silke Rottenberg, the first-choice keeper for the German women's team.

Her moment finally came in the 2007 Women's World Cup. Rottenberg was injured and Angerer was put into goal. It was the year that Germany won the Women's World Cup. Of course, it was lonely possible thanks to Angerer. She played in all six matches in China and didn't let a single goal past her.

That's 540 minutes of gameplay without conceding a goal. It was a new record, although as she said, "The whole tournament I wasn't thinking about it because I was so much under pressure. I was just focusing on not making any mistakes."

To appreciate the magnitude of this feat it's essential to understand that Germany played Brazil in the final. Brazil had torn apart all the opposing teams and scored an impressive 17 goals, but they couldn't get one past Angerer.

Of particular note was the penalty she saved in the closing moments of the game against Brazil. Their star striker, Marta, took her shot and Angerer dived halfway across the goal, just reaching it with her hand to knock it away. It didn't just keep her clean sheet, it secured Germany's victory. At the point of the penalty they were leading 1-0, if Angerer had let the goal in Germany may not have won the game or the cup!

As the news reported, she went from nobody to hero almost overnight.

That World Cup meant Angerer took over as first-choice goalkeeper for Germany. In 2009 and 2013 her skills again saved the day, allowing Germany to win the Women's European championships both times. This time, her amazing penalty-saving skills saved two penalty shots by Norway in the final.

This occasion was even more memorable as seven of the normal players were out of action due to injury. As the team captain, Angerer had to help select seven replacements, most of whom lacked experience. It was her leadership and motivation that ensured the team had a positive attitude and bonded well, culminating in winning the championship.

Her performance won her the Women's Ballon d'Or. Angerer is the only goalkeeper, male or female, to have ever won this award!

FUN FACTS ABOUT NADINE ANGERER

- Angerer was capped 145 times by the German national soccer team
- She was instrumental in winning the 2005 UEFA Women's Cup
- Angerer won the UEFA Woman's Championship on all five occasions she played
- She was named FIFA World Player of the Year in 2014
- She started out as a forward!

QUICK TRIVIA TEST

When was Angerer born?

November 1978

How many times did she play in the UEFA Women's Championship?

Play

Which season did she win the UEFA Women's Cup?

2004 – 2005 season

What record did she set at the 2007 FIFA Women's World Cup?

540 minutes of gameplay without conceding a goal

What position did she originally play?

Forward

FIVE LIFE LESSONS

1. Persevere no matter how bad it looks

Angerer spent nearly ten years in the shadow of Rottenberg. She was the reserve goalkeeper for the national team and rarely played. However, she persevered and, ultimately, got a break in 2007. That's when she went from being a nobody to a legend.

In short, persevere, it will be worth it in the end/.

2. Do what you love

Angerer may have developed her love of the beautiful game later than most. But, her passion was real. It was this that allowed her to endure ten years on the bench for Germany, and has always encouraged her to be better.

It's much easier to be the best version of yourself if you're doing something you love.

3. Put your team first

Angerer wasn't thinking about breaking a record when she played 540 minutes without conceding a goal. Nor was she thinking of herself when she motivated a young German team to win the 2013 Women's European Championships.

By putting her team first, she received glory. More importantly, the team got the result they wanted. Teamwork matters!

4. Keep your options open

Angerer has always chosen her own path. She decided against joining an American college soccer team, although later played for American teams. She also left the German league to experience soccer in Sweden, even if it was just for a year.

In short, she has always been open to options and selecting the ones that suit her best. It's helped her grow as a player and an individual.

5. Lead by example

This is something that everyone should do. Angerer has always been passionate, organized, and respectful on the field. Her actions inspire other soccer players to do the same, helping everyone to get the most from the game.

JOY FAWCETT
THE ORIGINAL SOCCER MOM

Joy Lyn Fawcett was born in 1968. Fawcett is her married name as she was born Joy Lyn Biefield. She is well known as one half of the formidable duo: Fawcett and Overbeck were an almost unbeatable force in the center of the United States defense.

She was born in Southern California and attended Edison High School in Huntington Beach, California. Unsurprisingly, she spent most of her free time outdoors and was very athletic.

Her interest in soccer stems back to her childhood years. Her brother was passionate about the sport and frequently knocked the ball around with her. She joined her high school team and helped them win four league championships!

She then went on to attend the University of California, Berkeley and played with their team. Impressively, she scored 23 goals in the 1987 season, it was and still is a record for the university.

Upon leaving university with her BA degree in Physical Education, she joined Ajaa America, a Manhattan Beach Club women's soccer team. Her efforts helped the team win the US Women's Amateur championship in 1991 and 1993. She was also instrumental in Ajax's first season in the Women's Premier Soccer League, the team played in it for the first time in 2001.

Her play didn't go unnoticed as the San Diego Spirit sought her out and signed her for the 2001 season. Unfortunately, due to falling pregnant early in the season, she missed most of the games.

It was here that she set another record, that of returning to the field just six weeks after giving birth.

That didn't stop her triumphant return in 2002. This was the season she played 19 games, more than any other player. 2003 was challenging for her as she incurred an ankle injury. She started playing again as soon as it healed and managed to feature in 18 games that season.

Fawcett established herself as a key component on the US national soccer team. It was more than just being part of the team. Fawcett was part of the US team that won the 1991 Women's World Cup. The event was held in China and was the first of its kind.

Impressively, she was the only member of the US women's national team to play all the minutes of every game at the 1995, 1999, and 2003 Women's World Cup. That's an impressive tribute to her defensive ability.

Equally impressive, is that when she retired from the US Women's National team, she was the highest-scoring defender.

She didn't just represent the US in four Women's World Cups. Fawcett was part of three US Olympic teams, although the team never won an Olympic gold.

Impressively, when she retired, she had 239 caps for the US women's soccer team. 54 of these caps were connected to the World Cup and Olympic events.

Interestingly, Fawcett was playing professionally during the 1996 Presidential elections. At that time suburban moms were defined as "soccer mums". Fawcett turned the term on its head as she actually played soccer, and played it well.

Fawcett may have retired from the game professionally but she is still actively involved on the field. Her role with Pure Game allows her to use soccer and other sports to teach children character, helping them develop into well-rounded individuals and potential soccer players.

FUN FACTS ABOUT JOY FAWCETT

- Her brother, Eric Biefield, played for the US men's national team
- Despite not being an attacker she scored 27 goals for the US team
- She was inducted into the Soccer Hall of Fame in 2009
- Fawcett has three children but that never stopped her from playing
- Her professional career lasted from 1987 to 2004, she was the first American to have a child and return to the national team

QUICK TRIVIA TEST

What name was Fawcett born with?

Joy Lyn Biefield

When was the first-ever Women's World Cup?

1991

What position did Fawcett play?

Defender

How many caps did she get for the US team?

239

What was she the first American to do?

Have a child and return to the national soccer team

FIVE LIFE LESSONS

1. Equality is real!

We live in a world that strives to create an equal environment for everyone. It's not always easy and women have struggled to gain the same rights as men in many arenas.

But, as Fawcett proves, change is possible, as is equality. It took until 1991 for women to have a World Cup tournament, today women's football is well-established and recognized across the globe.

2. Do it your way

Many people follow the herd, but Fawcett did it her own way. That's why she had such a long professional career and why she returned to the national team after giving birth.

Never be afraid to make your own decisions and do it your way. As she says "To do it, to go for it if that's what you love."

3. Hard work pays off

Fawcett didn't become one of the best female professional soccer players overnight. It took dedication and a love of the game. Her skill and ability to consistently improve allowed her to keep playing and write her own rules.

But, it took a lot of work and support, proving that hard work does pay off sooner or later.

4. Family matters

Fawcett had three children while playing professional soccer. She was a pioneer as being pregnant while playing sports at such a high level was unheard of before.

It took a lot of planning to take babies and children with her on various trips but she was determined to be the best mom possible and a great soccer player.

She used her teammates, husband, and even a nanny to help her remain close to her children, because, to her, family matters.

5. Be Curious

Being curious means you also want to know what is happening, what is possible, and what you're dealing with. It's a positive trait and one that should be encouraged. After all, a curious mind is active and more likely to find interesting solutions.

Fawcett was always curious, even if it wasn't always the best result. Her teammate Julie Foudry remembers "We were barefoot, and the lights went out to save electricity. Joy felt something crunch beneath her feet, and she felt the need to shine her flashlight on the floor. It was, I swear, a five-foot cockroach."

It may not have been pleasant but it sums up Fawcett's curiosity and thirst for knowledge.

SARAH ZADRAZIL
THE RECORD BREAKER

Sarah Zadrazil was born in February 1993 in Bad Ischl, a historical spa town in Austria. It's a lovely town. However, as many youngsters are keen to do, Zadrazil wasn't impressed. She was more concerned with her way out.

As a youngster, she had a passion for soccer. However, there weren't many opportunities for a girl to play soccer in her home town.

That didn't stop her, she simply joined the local club and played alongside the boys. She was the only girl in the team. Zadrazil feels this has helped to make her a better player. If she can stand up to the rough and tumble of men's soccer then women's soccer should be easier.

She was one of the youngest players but also one of the best, the boys welcomed her without issue. Many of their victories were attributed to her skill.

Zadrazil managed to get into college in the US. This allowed her to play for their women's team. She played for the East Tennessee State Buccaneers, which are located in the southeastern part of the US.

It was here she really started to shine. In her freshman year, she broke the record for single-season assists by a freshman. She was also named the Atlantic Sun Freshman of the Year.

In her second year, she scored eight times and assisted with another 11 goals. This gave her the 2013 Atlantic Sun Player of the Year award. She followed this by becoming the career leader in points, assists, and shots attempted for the college. It was this year she was first named to the Southern Region Second team.

Her final year saw her becoming part of the NSCAA All-Southern Region Third Team. She was named Southern Conference Player of the Year, the first player from East Tennessee State Buccaneers to ever win this award.

By the time she left ETSU, she had 48 assists, 11 game-winning goals, 213 shots attempted, and 106 shots on goal. She was a career leader, left an indelible mark on the college, and still managed to graduate with a degree in exercise science.

Zadrazil loved her time in America, particularly the fact that women's soccer was so accepted and played everywhere. As she said, every college has a women's team. That's a big difference from her home town experience.

After finishing college with such an impressive, and record-breaking run, she was offered a space by the Washington Spirit reserve team. She played with them in 2015 and was key to their successful W-League run, they won the championship.

Unfortunately, she wasn't drafted in the 2016 NWSL College draft. Instead, she chose to go to Portland Thomas FC's training camp.

This led to an offer from Turbine Potsdam, a well-established club in the Frauen Bundesliga. She stayed with the team for four seasons until 2020. It was while she was here that she won the first Austrian Footballer of the Year award.

She also won the 2018-2019 Salzburger Leonidas Sportwoman of the Year award, adding to her impressive collection of trophies.

From Turbine Potsdam she moved to Bayern Munich, another top club in the German Frauen Bundesliga. Her skills were instantly recognized as she was given the vice-captain position. She's recently extended her contract here and will be with them until at least 2026.

Bayern Munich is striving to create the best women's team possible and recognizes Zadrazil as a vital component in the midfield, particularly in a defensive role.

Zadrazil has also been selected to play for the Austrian national team on several occasions. She played her first game for the national team in 2010, they played Turkey but failed to beat them.

In 2016 she was a valuable member of the squad and even scored a goal in their 6-1 victory against Kazakhstan. The same year she was also instrumental in taking Austria to the final of the Cyprus Cup and winning it. Despite being primarily defense she scored once during the game.

The team also made it as far as the semifinal in the 2017 UEFA Women's Euro Championship.

Zadrazil is determined to get more women involved in soccer and help it become the most popular female sport in the world. As such, she is part of the WePlayStrong campaign. They promote soccer via social media and by using vlogs, thereby increasing people's awareness of women's football.

The campaign focuses on following female professional soccer players as they go about their daily lives, proving that she is an inspiration to everyone around her.

FUN FACTS ABOUT SARAH ZADRAZIL

- Zadrazil joined the Austrian national youth team while studying to be a kindergarten teacher.
- Zadrazil can ride a unicycle and juggle at the same time! It was initially a way to improve coordination and balance.
- She was Austrian Footballer of the Year in 2018. It was decided by a panel from the Bundesliga and this was the first time the award had ever been given!
- Zadrazil has a severe fear of spiders, she can't go near them! Considering the condition of some locker rooms it was a problem when first starting out.
- Her favorite food is dumplings and cheese. It's a traditional Austrian dish called Kasnocken.

QUICK TRIVIA TEST

Where was Zadrazil born?

Bad Ischl, Austria

Which year was she Austrian Footballer of the Year?

2018

What is Zadrazil scared of?

Spiders

How many seasons did Zadrazil play for Turbine Potsdam?

Four

Which team did she move to after Turbine Potsdam?

Bayern Munich

FIVE LIFE LESSONS

1. Find Your Own Opportunities

Zadrazil was eager to play soccer but there were few opportunities for girls when she was young. Fortunately, she found a way to play, by joining the boy's team.

It shows that anything is possible if you find your own opportunities.

2. Follow Your Dreams

It can often be hard to take a different route to your friends, even if it is doing what you love. Zadrazil remembers playing with the Austrian national youth team while studying and thinking "Football took a lot of time, and sometimes there were moments when I thought 'ok, time for an away game this weekend, my friends are all doing something else...' but it was always fun for me."

Soccer was her passion and she stuck to her dream, even if it felt like she was sometimes missing out on other things.

3. Share to inspire others

Zadrazil uses the magic of modern technology to inspire other women to play soccer. She'll post videos and vlogs on social media to help others see what her average day is like and that it's possible for anyone to do the same.

She tries to make sure the videos are accurate, showing that it can be both fun and hard work. Her aim is to show others that the sacrifices are worthwhile. That's true of anything in life.

4. Be the best you can be

Zadrazil always strives to be the best she can be. Kit's recognized by her team. As the manager has said "Her blend of athleticism and technical ability sets her apart, making her a force to be reckoned with in central midfield."

You should always strive to be the best you can be, it's nice, but not essential, when that effort is recognized.

5. Learn from every experience

Zadrazil once said "I would say that the biggest difference in football is that it is just super physical, a lot of kick and rush, and working hard. In Germany now, it's a more tactical and technical style of football. It's cool if you can combine both and I think it helped me a lot."

Not all experiences are great, but learning from them all will make you better at what you do, whether that's soccer or something else.

BONUS MATERIAL SOCCER

100 Affirmations To Build Confidence

1. I am capable of anything
2. I'm a champion
3. I never give up
4. Anything is possible
5. I start each day with a positive mindset
6. Failing is simply an opportunity to learn
7. I'm not afraid to fail
8. I listen to others
9. I welcome any challenge
10. Challenges are simply obstacles I've not yet overcome
11. I can overcome anything
12. My left foot is as important as my right
13. I'm fit and full of energy
14. I learn from my mistakes
15. I will work hard at everything I do
16. I will do something despite being afraid
17. My fear can be used to inspire me
18. I can and will do better
19. Losing gives me an opportunity to improve
20. Everything I do I do better than I did it before
21. Make the most of every opportunity
22. Nobody knows what will happen next, make the most of now
23. Live in the moment, the past can be learned from but it's gone
24. Everyone makes mistakes, learn and move on
25. I am worthy of being loved
26. I'm a good person
27. My opinion matters

28. I'm not afraid to express my point of view
29. I can forgive anyone
30. I am very focused
31. I am strong
32. I will train harder than my teammates
33. I am good at concentrating on one task
34. I am stronger every day
35. My attitude helps to get the best out of my teammates
36. I'm unstoppable
37. I will exceed other people's expectations, and my own
38. I can survive anything
39. I'm a natural athlete
40. I can make difficult decisions
41. I'm flexible
42. I can make quick decisions even under pressure
43. I will be the best that I can be
44. I trust my own abilities
45. I'm extremely disciplined
46. I believe in myself
47. I'm loved by family and friends
48. I love my family and friends
49. I am proud of the unique person I am
50. I deserve to be loved
51. I can make a difference
52. My body is perfect, just the way it is
53. I appreciate the natural beauty in the world around me
54. I can recover from any setback
55. I'm great at solving problems
56. I can think outside the box
57. I always treat others how I would like to be treated
58. Nothing is impossible
59. I'm passionate about learning new skills
60. I can always grow as a person
61. I'm excited about future prospects

62. I'm good at setting, and then achieving, goals
63. I understand and embrace my feelings
64. I'm capable of calming myself when angry
65. I learn from my mistakes without dwelling on the past
66. Every day is full of new and exciting prospects
67. I smile at everyone I meet
68. I'm grateful for what I have
69. I'm confident
70. I am proud of what I have achieved
71. I display empathy for others
72. I choose to be happy
73. Learning is a gift I unwrap every day
74. I'm a positive influence on everyone around me
75. I'm always open to new ideas
76. I'm intelligent
77. I stand up for others
78. I'm capable of defending my own opinions and actions
79. I can make my dreams come true
80. I am important
81. I make good decisions
82. I know the difference between right and wrong
83. I can handle responsibility
84. I'm a good role model
85. I understand the importance of boundaries and respect them
86. I like to include others
87. I'm a good team player
88. I believe curiosity is a blessing
89. I'm open to anything
90. I can be a great leader
91. I am appreciative of others
92. I make good things happen
93. I believe generosity will be rewarded

94. I enjoy helping others even when others don't appreciate my help
95. I trust my own instincts
96. Every opportunity is a bonus
97. I'm a great friend
98. I'm not perfect but nobody is
99. I have a fantastic personality
100. I know the importance of taking a break

The Mental Mindset To Help You Succeed At Soccer

As a budding soccer player, you want to win every time. This desire is important if you want to be professional and to be the best you can be. However, you can't win every game or every tackle. You may also come across other obstacles, such as injuries, personal or family issues, and even apparently unfair referees. To help you deal with these issues and come out the other side stronger and a better player, you need to develop mental resilience now.

Fortunately, just as practice can make you a better soccer player, practice can also help you create the right mental mindset for success.

Affirmations

The first step is to start believing in yourself and boosting your self-confidence. Affirmations, such as the 100 we've given you will help you boost your self-confidence. You don't need to read or repeat all the affirmations every day.

Instead, write them out and put them in a jar. Pull out one or two a day and state them over and over again throughout the day. If you say it enough times out loud you will start to believe. Self-confidence will help you overcome a lot of obstacles.

Face Your Emotions

Emotions can be powerful and they can easily derail your positive attitude. You need to learn how to deal with your emotions from an early age. It doesn't involve suppressing them! Instead, identify what the emotions are. You can then try breathing exercises or a simple soothing technique such as slowly counting to ten. To finish, as you calm down, share your emotion with someone you trust. It allows you to own it and learn from it.

Set Goals

To help you overcome obstacles and stay positive you need to know that you're capable of achieving anything. The simplest way to build this mindset is to set yourself goals. They should be achievable within a couple of weeks, achievable, but not too easy. This will make you work and appreciate what you've achieved. It also feels great and gives your confidence a real boost.

When you're challenged you can think about what you've already achieved and how you managed it. This will allow you to apply the same principles to future challenges.

Be A Team Player

If you want to play soccer you're going to be part of a team, that means you'll need to be a team player. This is a mindset which can be easily built by doing team events. Start by joining your family doing things, then move on to joining local teams, they don't have to be soccer-related. The more involved you are with other people the easier you'll find it to be part of a team.

Acknowledge There Is Always More To Learn

No one knows everything, there is always something else you can learn. Understanding this is important to ensure you have the mental fortitude to learn from your mistakes. It's the only way you can get better at what you do.

To practice this, you need to listen to others when they criticize, and even be open to asking people how they think you could have done it better. It can be painful listening to honest opinions. However, identifying the issues can help you address them and improve as a player and a person. The sooner you seek out criticism and use it to help you improve, the easier you'll find it in the future.

Young Persons Guide To Playing Soccer

You're never too young to start kicking a ball around and developing your soccer skills. Developing a passion and a talent for the game is a great first step toward playing soccer professionally. Of course, you don't have to be professional to enjoy playing. But, you do need it understand the rules.

The Teams

Professional soccer teams play on a field which is at least 110 yards long and 70 yards wide. In fact, most teams in the US have fields which are 115 yards long and 75 yards wide!

There's a circle marking the center of the field and rectangles with semi-circles surrounding each goal, these are the penalty zones. A penalty kick mark will be positioned inside them.

Each team consists of 11 players, one of whom is the goalkeeper. The others are forwards, midfielders, and defenders. The exact number of people in each position will depend on the team manager and which setup they believe will be most beneficial. The 4-3-3 format is the most popular, it's where there are four defenders, three midfielders, and three forwards.

Of course, all teams have more players so that they can be switched on and off the field as necessary. Youth teams tend to play on a smaller field so they may have fewer players.

Equipment

Soccer equipment is surprisingly simple. When playing on grass all players wear soccer boots with studs on. These help to provide grip. The studs aren't necessary when playing on artificial surfaces.

Players will always wear shin pads to protect their shins from accidental kicks. Other than that, long socks, shorts, and a jersey with the team name and player number are all that's needed. The goalkeeper is allowed to wear gloves as they may need to save the ball with their hands. They are the only player allowed to touch the ball with their hands.

Playing Basics
A solid white line defines the edge of the field. If the ball passes this line then it's out of play. Whichever team touched it last gives possession to the opposite team.

Each game is 90 minutes long. Play is separated into two halves, each 45 minutes long. There is normally a 15-minute break between the two halves of the game.

If injuries and offenses stop the game the clock isn't stopped. Instead, the referee keeps track of the lost time and adds it on at the end. It's referred to as stoppage time. For tournament games, should the game be tied at the end of stoppage time, it will go into 30 minutes of extra time. If it's still tied there will be a penalty shootout. In this instance, both teams get five penalties, the one that scores the most wins.

Rules To Be Aware Of
While playing soccer you need to be aware of the rules. Breaking these can lead the referee to give you a warning, a yellow card, or a red card. A warning is for a very minor offense, a second warning automatically becomes a yellow card.

Yellow cards are issued for minor offenses, but two yellow cards is the same as a red card. Red cards are issued for serious offenses and result in you being instantly sent off the field. Your team has to continue without you and one player less on the field.

It's worth noting that four players can be sent off with a red card. If a fifth is sent off then the game will end and the side with five red cards will automatically lose.

Other rules you need to know before playing are:

- **Offside**

A player can be anywhere on the field. However, if you receive the ball or can interfere with play, and you were in front of the ball with only the goalkeeper and one defender between you and the goal, you'll be offside and the opposing side will be given a free kick.

- **Fouls**

When tackling another player they must have the ball. The tackle should be clean and you should target the ball, not the player. If you push, trip, or even hold the other player you will be fouling them. The referee will decide if you deserve a warning or a yellow/red card and the opponents will get a free kick.

- **Penalties**

If the foul happens when the opposite team is attacking and they are inside the penalty area by your goal, then the referee can choose to give them a penalty. The ball is put on the penalty spot and one player from the opposing team takes a shot. Your goalkeeper needs to save it!

Getting Started

You can start playing soccer at any age. Focus on learning to kick the ball exactly where you want it to go. That's essential for passing and shooting. Passing is particularly important for midfielders, defenders, and goalkeepers!

You can also try dribbling, simply kicking the ball and keeping it close to your feet as you move around obstacles as fast as you can.

When you're ready, join your local youth club and start practicing with them regularly. Remember, the more you practice, the better you'll get. Practicing with a club will also give you the opportunity to sample different positions. This can help you decide where you are most comfortable and where your skills fit best. Not everyone is a natural forward, goalkeepers are just as important!

Made in the USA
Las Vegas, NV
15 December 2024

14382824R00075